M000290451

STANDING
THROUGH IT ALL

TONYA ALSTON

© Copyright 2020 - Tonya Alston

All Rights Reserved.

ISBN: 978-0-578-64741-8

No part of this book may be reproduced or transmitted in any form or by any means; graphic, electronic, or mechanical, including photocopying, recording, taping or by any information storage retrieval system without written permission of the author.

Printed in the United States of America

Dedication

I dedicate this book to my beautiful daughter Britney Victoria Alston, thank you for being my best friend, there when I obtained my High School Diploma, Undergraduate Degree, International Masters in Business Administration and Master in Theology. Your love helped me, not to give up and has resulted in me being the woman that I am today; CEO of two companies and the Founder of the Nonprofit Healing the Living. You made me drive harder to the finish line. Your relationship with Jesus encouraged me to pray and study God's word more! In memory of my loving mother, Edith Mae Stevens, I feel like I know more about you now than ever before. When I see my hands, I see your hands. You would be proud, I love you (September 22, 1938 -September 9, 2004). To the Lovely Mrs. Hazel, "Jody" Lindsey, thank you for being there for me when I was growing up. May God continue to bless you. To my Godparents, God knew what I needed long before it happened. You have both been a Mother, Father and grandparents offering love and support to me and my daughter. I love you.

Table of Contents

Forward

Reading the story of this author was nothing short of being a testimony of overcoming life obstacles and challenges. The author should not have made it to write this book. I can relate to her story of being physically and spiritually abused. Not many women nor people would have the strength to describe in detail what she went through. Church is supposed to be a safe place where you are strengthened, refreshed and restored. Knowing and seeing how successful she is today; I would never had known that she had such a dark past. The story led me through her life's journey, and I found her words liberating and therapeutic. This book will change someone's life and let them know they can make it, no matter what and through it all.

Cheryl Edwards

Chapter 1

BORN

Standing 5' 8" inches tall with skin the color of caramel, high cheek bones, a smile of perfect pearly whites crowned with a gold tooth; my mother lit up every room that she entered. She was the life of any party and quite the social butterfly, but she didn't have it easy. Born to a mother who could not read nor write, she was lost in the education system and dropped out of school in the sixth grade. She relied heavily on her looks for most of her life. Pregnant at 17 years old by a young man that took her virginity without her consent. Yes, she was a rape victim and gave birth to her firstborn child, a son. She was quite the tomboy at that time, hanging out with the guys and playing basketball. No one would believe her, not her mother nor her aunts. It was a shame that she buried and carried with her for the remainder of her life.

Later, relocating from North Carolina to Washington DC at full blossom, she had another son. The second son would find himself in constant trouble, landing him in prison for most of his life. At a very young age, he was tricked by a group of older men to sneak into an electronic store and help them rob the place. He was arrested and after going before the judge, he was placed on permanent probation. The sentence resulted in him going back to jail every time he would do something wrong, which was often.

My mother ran a strict house; first, it must be clean, and we are not talking about average cleaning, but the type of cleaning that after the beds were made no one could sit on them. I can hear her voice clearly, "Go outside!" and I would stay outside until it was time for dinner. Often, depending on her mood, I would hear her call my name from the window while I was outside playing, and when I would answer, she would simply say, " Can you get me a glass of water." This was apparently the norm for all the kids in the neighborhood. Their parents would do the same, so I didn't feel bad.

Finding love, could he be the one? Tall, dark, and handsome. He must be the one, a man willing to marry my mother and raise both of her sons. This marriage was not what she expected for her first love. It turned out to be an abusive relationship, both physically and verbally. Her husband did not respect her sons, and while she was hard at work to support her children now two sons and now a daughter, he would entertain women at night in their home. Yes, you heard me right, a daughter. She had a daughter by her first husband.

One night her firstborn managed to get out the closet to call her on the phone. He let her know what her husband had been doing and that there was a woman in the house. After arriving home earlier than expected, she found the doors locked from the inside. In desperation, she climbed through the window, only to find her husband in their marital bed with another woman. Furious, she snapped, getting her gun and shooting at them both. She barely missed his heart, sending her husband to the hospital. The fury would not go without punishment as she found herself behind bars facing an attempted murder charge. When it was time to appear before a judge, she quickly learned what it meant to be favored by God, the Judge found her not guilty, and she was released. It was a crime of passion, and she was out of her mind at that moment. Unfortunately, she remained in the relationship and found herself being abused verbally on a regularly basis. My mother worked hard to support the family and would have to hide money to buy clothes and shoes for the children. Being the dishonoring man that he was known to be, he would find the money and spend it on other things. They struggled, living in an inner-city low-income area, that was ridden with drugs and violence. She would try to return to her faith, having been raised Catholic for a brief time she began trusting God. Her husband would make jokes about her relationship with God as he was an atheist and did not believe. Later he was diagnosed with throat cancer and ended up having his tongue cut out of his mouth before passing. It makes you wonder, could this be a result of his mocking God? Indeed, he must not have heard about God's anger shown in the old testament days!

Life goes on, she meets someone else and has a baby girl. This person was not relevant as she never spoke much about him. I imagine it was intimate moments that ended up with a positive pregnancy test. This daughter was very fair-skinned and so beautiful that I was told that her family and friends would ask, "Whose baby is that?" It was definitely her child, but she was different from the other children in ways that she learned more about later in life.

Her charm and smile never failed her because she finds herself in love again… Mr. Tall, Dark, and Handsome. This one was different, and she would end up spending many years with him as he was the love of her life. He helped raise the children, now two sons and two daughters but not without conflict. They remained in an on and off again relationship for over nine years. Determined not to have any more children, when she found herself pregnant, it was soon terminated at an illegal abortion clinic. The abortion left her physically damaged. After some years, she experienced a miscarriage and loss of a child. Now she had her hands full with four young children, living in the housing projects, and her mother helped babysit from time to time. It became so frequent that they called my mother by her first name and my grandmother, ma. During this time, men were not allowed to live with the women in the projects, so my grandmother asked the love of her daughter's life to move out. This was difficult because he had become a staple in the home, a father to her children. Marriage was never discussed, but she loved him dearly. One day she had this gut feeling that something wasn't right. The man that she so dearly loved started to treat her differently, after moving out, so she decided to take the last of her bus fare and pay him a visit. When she arrived, she saw him before he saw her. He was coming down the street with another woman. Shocked when he saw my mother, they began to argue, and out of hurt, my mother tried to fight him. During the scuffling, he snatched the $500 wig off her head that he had purchased. Embarrassed, she left and didn't see him for a few months. As the year was coming to an end, feeling lonely, she decided to pay him a visit. When she knocked on the door, she found him with the same woman, but to her surprise, this was more serious than she thought, the woman was pregnant. Apparently, this relationship had started even before my grandmother had asked him to move out. Did my grandmother know? Did she have a gut feeling?

Working day and night, determined to get out of the system and out the projects. My mother had gotten a job with the Federal Government as an elevator operator. Yes, there was such a thing as someone standing in the elevator to take you to your desired floor. Standing tall and more beautiful than ever, she meets a young man. He was formally in the Navy, college-educated, and would pick her up for dates in a shiny silver Cadillac. He spoiled her by inviting her out to fine restaurants and taking her shopping. She had never experienced a relationship like this before. She was always the responsible one in the relationship. After dating for a while, this young man from Greensboro, N.C. would ask her to marry him. Accepting, they were married at the courthouse in Arlington VA, which was different from her first marriage, where she wore a light blue wedding dress and was a stunning bride. Marrying allowed her access to his military benefits and a different way of life. As time went on, she began to gain weight and went to the doctor as she believed that she was pregnant, only to be told that she was not pregnant. Months went by, and she returned, demanding that they give her a rabbit test, which is what they called a pregnancy test in those days. Sure enough, she was pregnant and six months at that! This was supposed to be a happy time, but her newly married husband wasn't the picture-perfect man after all. He had a lot to hide, and she soon found herself in another violent relationship, but this time she was pregnant. She confronted him one day after she went for a check-up and learned that he had given her a sexually transmitted disease. Concerned about her unborn child, "Me that is," the conversation turned violent in the car, and her husband pulled a gun out on her. She opened the door of the moving car and jumped out. Clearly, the car wasn't moving at high speed because she and the baby were fine. But as history repeats itself, she did not leave.

"I made it, I'm finally here!" **BORN** December 4, 1972, to cold weather, bell-bottoms, and afros. When I arrived, I broke the mold. My mother had two sons, two daughters, and yes, I was number five. I once heard a Woman of God say that five was the number of grace. "Yes, I was meant to be here." After my oldest sister was born, my mother was told by an elderly lady that she would one day have two brown-skinned daughters. Her second daughter was very fair, and after an abortion, a miscarriage, and years later, I arrived. My mother said that I was the most challenging delivery that she ever had to endure. She did not understand that where there is pain, there is purpose. "Yes, I said it." She was birthing purpose! Jeremiah 1:5 "Before I formed you in the womb, I knew you, and before you were born, I consecrated you; I appointed you a prophet to the nations." (English Standard Version). This scripture is so profound, it tells me that before my mother met my father that I was somewhere in heaven with God, and he knew me before he released me into this earth.

It was all a dream, a baby girl. The house was filled with constant laughter and visitors welcoming me into this world. Little did we know that the smiles would be short-lived. Just three months later, while visiting her mother in North Carolina, my grandmother ran into a friend of hers. As she bragged to her friends about her new grand-baby and my father, there was utter confusion when she found out that he was married to another woman. It seemed that Mr. Tall, Dark, and Handsome was in love with the idea of getting married. My mother found herself in a marriage that would end while holding her three-month-old baby girl. What would she do?

Chapter 2

Started from the Bottom

Police sirens, Ambulances, and the nearly unbearable smell of urine was our new way of life. All-day, there was yelling, loud music, and people talking late at night in the hallways into the early morning. Our hallway was the most popular because we now lived in a basement apartment. It was dark, damp, and the location that homeless people and drug addicts used to urinate. It was nothing like where we lived before, but it was what my mother could afford. My siblings were a lot older than me and were all caught up in the new era of sex and drugs. My mother had three heroin addicts on her hands. She continued to work and started taking me across town to the sitter, after learning that I was locked in the closet for hours as my sibling invited friends over to get high. My mother would tell me how she would find needles behind the couch. I imagine she was pretty down and out at this point. Five children, with different fathers and just when my mother thought she was finished. Behold, she has a baby girl. She needed help...

The sister born before me would spend most of her life with my grandmother's sister, my mother's aunt. She had a war going on within herself. As a little girl, I understand that she played with dolls with her first cousins, and as she started to get older, she began to identify more with being a boy than a girl. It was also my understanding that she was born with both body parts. As a woman, she better identified with a man, so she dressed and looked like a man. My cousin said that my sister began to identify as a man after spending time with a neighbor who was a lesbian. Unlike most babies born like her, the parents will generally decide the sex for the child, but in her case, my mother did not.

Now living in the slums, my mother escaped by playing cards and drinking with her friend's upstairs in the building. We would be there so long that I recall watching the sunrise. There was a lot of laughter, drinking, and smoking. The smoke was like a thick fog that would make my eyes water. This was our life night after night. Falling asleep on the couch and not waking up until the next day, became the norm for me. There was one house that we seemed to always visit more than others. I will never forget the green door with the bullet holes. We started to visit, even when there were no card games. My mother started dating an older man in the building. He was twenty years older than her, and we spent a lot of time with him. Sadly, to say, that green door is painted in my mind, along with late nights while sleeping in the living room, listening to the sirens and ambulances. It was difficult for me not to think about the story that I he told me when I asked where the bullet holes had come from. He said that a big green monster tried to break in, and he shot at it with his gun. All night, I would lay on the couch, scared that this creature would come back to get me. We began to stay there so much that we eventually moved in with him. Soon I was used to the noise at night and didn't care much about the door. During the day, I would play with some of the other kids in the back alley, which was full of glass and other things left behind by the nightwalkers.

My oldest brother had gone to the military, and I would only see my other siblings from time to time. A few years had gone by, and my mother was still going strong, with her new man. He wasn't Tall, Dark or Handsome. Instead, he was shorter than her, dark and could stand to lose a few pounds, but it was obvious that he loved my mother. When he saw her coming, he would smile bright with his gold tooth sparkling. It was evident that she felt the same, she seemed happy. At night they would play cards with their friends, and then I would hear them behind the green door laughing and cursing. They cursed way too much for my ears. During the era of gold teeth, afros, and bell bottoms. They were alike, he was the ying to her yang with matching gold teeth.

Given that I had so much time alone, I became fascinated with the fire alarms. I realized that if you pulled the alarm that the fire trucks and ambulances would come to the building, and all the people would run out of their apartments. So, I pulled it one too many times until my mother finally realized that it was me. I will never forget this day as it was the first spanking that I recalled receiving. I never knew that it wouldn't be my last. After that, I realized that I needed to find something else to do besides pulling the alarm. It was a long week on punishment, and I received a spanking that I would never forget.

My brother had returned home, and I remember how happy and excited my mother was to see him. He would stop by and visit, but soon, we would be moving on. My mother, me, and her boyfriend took a trip to Wilson, North Carolina. A small rural country town where my mother was born and raised. There were corn, cotton, and tobacco fields growing all around. At night it was completely dark, you didn't see streetlights and could barely see your hand in front of your face. What I didn't know is that while we were visiting, my mother was making plans. Her new man had proven just how much he loved her and me for that matter. I was happy because he had been the only stable man in my life from three months old. Now, he was building my mother a house in a new suburban neighborhood. He was not the type of man that she was used to dating. This man was different and put us first. Yes, us because we were a package deal.

On the way back to Washington, DC, I remember sleeping in the car for most of the trip. We started to visit regularly while the house was being built. I had family there, my grandmother and her sisters, so I enjoyed the visits. I loved my grandmother, she was like this big fluffy pillow, and I enjoyed naps across her lap. I always knew when we were back in the city without looking out the car window because of the bumpy roads and sounds of blowing horns. People were yelling across the streets when we pulled up. My mom was still the ultimate social butterfly. She would step out the car, and there it was, that smile with her gold tooth shining bright. The people in the neighborhood loved her, and she knew everybody.

We would quickly return to our regular routine, night after night. Cards, alcohol, and cigarettes. The smoke would fill the house, and unfortunately, there was nowhere for me to go because I didn't have my own bedroom. The one-bedroom in the house didn't have a television, so it was better to sit in the living area and endure the smoke. Will this ever end, I wondered?

By this time, my oldest brother was married, and they would stop by from time to time. I still love the pictures from his wedding day, everything then seemed perfect. My mother was beautiful, and I had on a lovely dress. I don't recall visits from my oldest sister, but I do remember the sister born before me. Still, it was like I was an only child, I always felt alone. Playing in the alley with whatever or whoever was available. Cursing, yelling, sirens, and the smell of urine all became part of my typical day. It was nothing like when we went to the country.

Coming home from the Vietnam war, the drug problem that my oldest brother had was only exacerbated. I heard stories from my mother how he would beat his wife and neglect her needs. My mother said that she would have to purchase her items like sanitary napkins and things that she needed. When his wife became pregnant, the beatings didn't stop, and my mother explained how she had to pull him off her one day. His wife loved him dearly, although I've heard his side of the story, he said she was a cheater. Even if she cheated on him, she was also the one who took him to get help. She found a lady who had church out of her home that helped change his life. This lady helped him get off drugs by introducing him to her version of God. A radical God who we only hear about in the Old Testament. A God that dealt with sin with an iron fist and not with love. Her teaching made him radical as well in his beliefs and teachings. My mother would say that he was in a cult because we never saw him much after. His wife soon left him and moved to California with their little girl. He didn't stay in touch with them and would say that the little girl wasn't his. Besides, this wasn't the first time that he said that a child wasn't his. This was his third child. He had a son that was born a year before my mother had given birth to me and a few years later, a daughter. She was born with his reddish-brown hair and light-colored eyes. My brother seemed to ignore the fact that he had these beautiful children and went on with his life.

Chapter 3

We Got Out!

Nearly a year later, I was almost five at the time when we were finally making the big move. Thick green grass is all that I could see for miles. When we pulled into the driveway. I couldn't believe it. This was out of the norm. At that age, I thought we had pulled up to the largest house in the world. With the most massive trees and greenest grass. There were neighbors, children riding their bicycles and playing dodge ball. It was nothing like the dark, wet, smelly alleyways that I was used to. At night, I saw stars in the sky for the first time in my life. I would raise my widow and peer out for hours at a time. There was no yelling, sounds of sirens, nor ambulances. The only thing that I could hear was the sound of crickets and frogs. This was a new beginning.

I soon met friends in the neighborhood, but it wasn't easy. Everyone looked at me like I was so different because they said that I talked funny. My first friendship started with an altercation. She was telling me how to pronounce pork and beans. Apparently, in Wilson, they pronounced it Pokinbeens. We went back and forth until we ended up in a fight. When it was all over, we became the best friends

21

ever. I was a city girl in a country town. My mother's boyfriend did not move with us right away. He remained in Washington until he retired from his job. Every weekend until I was almost nine years old, we would travel to Washington. If we didn't go there, he would come to Wilson. When we arrived, it was back to the way that it was. Smoking and more drinking! The loud noises, the screaming, and the smoke had started to burn my eyes. I began to hate the trips back and forth, but without fail on Fridays, my mother would show up to the school and check me out early. We would catch the train and head back to what I use to consider home. I now preferred the country accents, the opportunity to escape the card parties, and finally, I had my own room.

There were no more alleys, we had a huge front and backyard. My mother bought me a swing set for the backyard. This was much better than the rusted swing sets in the Washington DC parks. I seldom went to that park because it was mostly a hangout for the homeless and those that needed somewhere to get high. Now I could swing as long as I wanted. I would see beautiful butterflies and hear the birds sing. I remember the first time that I saw a red bird and learned that it was called a Red Robin. Which what considered the North Carolina State bird. I could not believe my eyes. I know that all of this may seem so insignificant for you, but for me, WE GOT OUT!

Being the only child, I didn't have any say as to whether I wanted to go back to the city. I also learned to obey whatever my mother asked me to do because if I didn't, I had quickly learned the consequences. Although my mother was four hours away from her boyfriend, they managed to make it work. He seemed genuinely happy to see her when we arrived, but I questioned if my mother was happy to see him. I really couldn't tell. Her smile seemed to fade as the years went on. Was he just our ticket out? Did she really love this man? He wasn't anything like her first nor second husband. He worked for the government and spent most of his time in the underground tunnels of DC working in the sewage. He always seemed dirty to me, and when he would laugh, his breath was awful. I know his breath could raise the dead! I felt wrong about thinking this way because, as I've said before, he was good to us and the reason I now have my own bedroom. When we would come into town, my siblings would come and visit from time to time, but they wouldn't stay long.

Back in North Carolina, my mother soon met new drinking and card buddies. Instead of having people over, this time, we would drive to someone else's house where there were even more people than when we had card parties in Washington DC. The one thing that did not change is that they would still play until the sun came up. This house had a bar inside, and no matter what time of day we went over, it was always full of people. I learned later in life that it was a liquor house. Going there wasn't that bad, it was a relatively large house, and there was somewhere for me to go. I did not have to sit in a smoke-filled room, listening to the adults' curse. There were also other kids that I could watch tv and play board games with. It seemed that my mother started drinking a lot more than before. She drank, and she slept. When she wasn't sleeping, she was drinking and playing cards. I wasn't used to her being like this because she was always the most social out of everyone.

Chapter 4

The Unforgotten

Look, everyone! Give Tonya a hand, she's got a new hairdo. Everyone in the class clapped and smiled, but it made me very sad. What everyone didn't know was that I had been dressing myself for school. No one had cared for my needs for some time now. I would try to do my own hair, but how well could a seven-year-old really take care of themselves. There was no one to tell me to brush my teeth nor take a proper bath. I will never forget this day. Something that was so innocent and meant to be a compliment has lived with me even until now as a day of great pain and sadness. This was the day my self-esteem began to slowly chip away.

My best friend's mom asked if she could do my hair. For the first time for nearly a year, my hair was done by someone other than me. On the outside, no one would think that I was taking care of myself because I always had beautiful clothes, but I didn't have the love, nor attention. When I would leave for school, my mother would be sleep. I would get up, dress, and head next door to my best friend's house for breakfast. Her mom would always cook them a warm breakfast before school. She would always make sure that she had enough for me too.

Finally, we had stopped going to Washington so frequently, and I started to look forward to the weekends, not because of Saturdays, but Sundays were the most exciting for me. Every Sunday, a lady name Sister Saul would drive through the neighborhood and pick up all the children that she could fit in her brown station wagon. She would pick us up for Sunday school. I would make sure that I got up early to get dressed and would stand, waiting at the screen door. My mother would be sleep, but when I would arrive home, she would be awake back in her spot drinking and smoking her cigarettes. I don't know what happened to her. This move was supposed to change our lives for the better. I was sure that things would be better, our life had changed drastically. We were no longer living in a basement apartment with hallways that smelled of urine, people yelling, and the sound of constant slamming doors. Now we had a new beautiful home with a huge front and back yard. Something was wrong with my mother; I couldn't understand why she was so unhappy.

When my mother wasn't sleeping, she was hanging curtains, and constantly redecorating the house. We had a lovely home now, one of the best in the neighborhood. The neighborhood had no streetlights and was pitch dark, so my mother put up the first streetlight in the community in our back yard. She would still play her music while she cooked and sang. Did I say my mother was a fantastic cook? Everyone would want to come over to eat when my mother cooked. Like all kids, there were some things that she would cook that I didn't like. When she would cook food that I didn't like, I could always depend on my best friends bother to eat it for me. It seemed that everything was looking up for us, so it was hard for me to understand why she is so unhappy. I would try to make her happy sharing with her my success in school. Although my self-esteem was low, I was an excellent student. I would always receive awards, but there would be no one at the award ceremonies to support me. The principal would call my name and say, "Please remain standing."

I remember coming home one day while my mother was hanging a new set of curtains. As I tried to tell her what happened at school and that my name was in the newspaper, she yelled, "Don't you see that I am busy!" But I persisted, she turned and swung the hammer at me. I ducked as I had quickly learned that reflex after having dishes thrown at me and wet dish rags swung at my face. I ran in my room where I now spent most of my time and cried. I would cry and talk to my imaginary friend.

Every Sunday, I would wait for Sister Saul to pick me up for Sunday School. After church, I would tell my mother how much I loved going there and that she should go with me one day. Every Sunday, she would say maybe next time. I just wanted her to smile again. She seemed angry all the time now. I would get spankings for reasons that I wasn't aware of and told to go to my room. It was so much better when I didn't have a bedroom, I started to miss the dark, smelly alleyways. Now it seems that I am always in my room. While in my room, I would play and continue talking to my imaginary friend. It didn't seem so imaginary then because we would talk and talk. Sometimes I would cry and ask why didn't my mother love me? I would draw pictures and write momma I am sorry that I am so bad. Over time, I had become such a sad child. My best friend would come and play with me in my room when she knew that I wasn't able to go outside. She had become like a sister to me.

On report card day, I would stand at the bus stop in fear of going home if I had received a B on my report card. I knew that wasn't going to be good enough for my mother and that I would receive a spanking in addition to harsh punishment. Sometimes if I was punished and my best friend couldn't come inside, she would talk to me outside of my screen window.

The days that I wasn't on punishment was spent playing with the kids in the neighborhood. Everyone chose to hang out and play at the end of our street because it was a dead-end. We would race, play kickball, basketball, and hide and seek. Unlike the children of today, we would play from sunup to sundown!

The best time of the year for me was the summer. No, it wasn't because we were out of school, I loved school, it was because I went away. My father, who was originally from Greensboro North Carolina, was only two hours away from where we lived. Every summer, my grandfather would pick me up on the last day of school, and I started spending my summers in Greensboro. When I would get home on the last day of school, my grandfather retired from the military and the postal service would be waiting for me in his car, smiling from ear to ear. Oh, how I loved him! Those were the best times for me because it was an escape. My father's family was well educated and Christian. In the summers, I wasn't allowed to watch television, I was taught how to crochet and make paper dolls. My grandmother was an amazing artist. She would draw the people, and I would make their clothes. I had a bicycle there and would ride through the neighborhoods. I would spend time with my grandparents, but my father would only be there, maybe on the day that I arrive, and I wouldn't see him after that. That didn't bother me much because I received so much love from my grandparents and my dearest aunt.

Growing up, I often wished that she was my mother. While away, they made sure that my hair was washed and styled appropriately. I had regular baths and timely meals. Remember I said my mother was a great cook, but nowadays it was when she wanted to cook… My dearest aunt would take me to museums and watch while I would crochet, making sure that I understood the craft. She was also part of the first sorority that you will learn more about after I write my story. I recall being on campus with her and her sisters. They wore pink and green walking with dignity across the campus yard.

It always seems like the summers went too fast! Soon, they were over, and it was time for me to return home. I would soon be turning nine years old. As I mentioned, our trips to Washington weren't weekly, but we would still go from time to time. This was one of those weekends. On our trip, this time, it seemed different. Apparently, the man that had been so good to us started to act different and distant. When we arrived, he told my mother that he had to work, but my mother found out that he wasn't working at all. My mother, if you recall me mentioning, had a temper that landed her in jail for almost killing her first husband. On this visit, my mother found her man two floors up in the apartment with another woman. I remember seeing a side of my mother that I have never seen before. She was in rage! She banged and banged on the door until he finally opened the door. She pushed him out of the way and yelled at me, "Go back to the apartment!" Of course, I didn't listen, I went down one level and stood in between the stairwell. I heard yelling, cursing, crashing, and my mother heading to the door. I quickly ran back to the apartment, now I feared that I was next. So, I just started to cry. When I saw her, she was crying and looked at me and said, "Let's go"! We went over to my great aunt's house, who also lived in Washington, DC, and soon caught the train back home.

Chapter 5

Changed!

For the next week, she mostly drank and slept. The following Sunday, as usual, I got dressed and waited for Sunday School. When I arrived home, I recall going directly to the china cabinet and pulling out this picture of Jesus showing the way to a man that had been in the military. I took this picture to my mom, and she just started to cry. I then began to tell her about Sunday School and to please go with me. The next Sunday, when Sister Saul arrived, it wasn't just me; my mother was dressed as well. We drove to the church on this day, and after attending Sunday School, we participated in the morning church service. When we returned home, my mother could not stop crying. This time the tears seemed different and continued throughout the week. I called Sister Saul on the phone and explained to her that she had been crying ever since she left the church. She came over and talked with my mother.

Something happened this day. My mother stopped drinking, stopped smoking, and got rid of everything that resembled her life before the day. From what I know now, it was extreme, but she was determined. She was also a music lover and had all types of records that would play while she drank and played cards with friends. I saw her placing them in bags and throwing them all away. The next weekend she was with me, and we were headed to church. The following weekday, her boyfriend that she had just had the horrible fight with showed up at the house. I saw them talk and he left, but the next weekend, he returned. We dressed in all white, my mother was getting married! It wasn't a big wedding; we went to the courthouse. But I saw her smile again, was this it? This couldn't be why everything has changed so drastically. What I soon learned is that she had given her life to Christ. A prayer that we had all been taught to pray in Sunday school. According to Roman 3:23 ESV For all have sinned and fallen short of the glory of God, and are justified by his grace as a gift, through redemption that is in Christ Jesus. My mother had been redeemed!

Salvation, my mother had prayed the prayer of salvation, called the Roman's Road. The Roman Road goes something like this: Dear Load Jesus, I know that I am a sinner, and I ask for Your forgiveness. I believe You died for my sins and rose from the dead. I turn from my sins and invite You to come into my heart and life. I want to trust and follow You as my Lord and Savior. Praying this prayer when you really want God to change your life, is life changing. I watched God change my mother's life this day. She didn't struggle like most of us, she was Changed! From this point forward, instead of being at the liquor house where she would drink and play cards, we spent our time in every church service. Whenever the doors were open, we would be there. One of my great aunts was a very well-known Pastor who had two churches in the Wilson area. This was not the norm during this era for an African American, especially for a woman to Pastor and especially not a large church. Women Pastors were controversial then and remain controversial, even today.

Instead of going to Sister Saul's church with my friends who I had grown to love and looked forward to seeing on Sundays would soon be in my past. We would attend my great aunt's church on Sundays. During the week, we would visit Sister Saul's church for nightly service. My time spent in a church was frequent. We would attend Tuesday night bible study and Friday night prayer meeting. If there was a traveling evangelist anywhere near Wilson, we found ourselves taking the drive there. The tents were often sweltering and did not have bathrooms only porta potties that you did NOT want to use because the smell was horrible. We would fill an empty plastic milk gallon container with water and freeze it for those trips. My mother would fry chicken for sandwiches, which were the highlight for me.

After my mother was saved or accepted Christ as her savior, everyone in the neighborhood knew that she was different. She began to share with others, and soon my best friend's father was also saved. The church became part of all our lives.

My mother's now-husband was still in Washington DC but finally getting close to coming to live with us. He was still working his government job until he could retire. Although they were married, he did not change his old habits. He would drink and still enjoy his card parties. We didn't visit anymore and would wait until he came to visit us. My great aunt from Washington would come down for the holidays, and my mother would cook an enormous amount of food. Everyone would have such a fantastic time. My grandmother, who they called Big Eve and for a reason, loved the food the most. She was an incredible woman to me. She never talked much, and it was said that it was because in her younger years that she had killed a man with her bare hands, choking and lifting him up off the floor. See, she didn't have an easy life either.

My grandmother was the firstborn of thirteen siblings who were a mixed nationality African and American Indian. Being the firstborn, she took on the responsibility of the family by helping with her siblings. She was never allowed to attend school. My grandmother was a victim of rape at the age of thirteen, which was an unlucky number for her.

She gave birth to a son, does this sound familiar? Generational curse maybe… Because she was so young, her son was given to a family member to raise as she went about her life. Later in life, she had another child, that died from premature death. She had left the baby with her sister, who now lives in Washington, DC, and the baby was given spoiled milk by accident and never recovered.

My grandmother was also partially deaf. She would sit with her beautiful silver, grey hair that she wore in two long braids that landed on her chest. Big Eve seldom dressed up in anything other than her house dresses, and you all think Madea was the first. Not! When she did, she would be very well coordinated with a dress and matching hat that she would tuck her beautiful, silver locks in. When I would go over to her house, she would always keep bananas for me. I liked them partly green before they started to ripe. When I was much younger, I recall having been left there by my mom, and I was extremely bored. I had to be about six or seven at the time. I started checking mailboxes that were on the street. Coming from the city, we didn't have mailboxes that you can open and look inside. I found what I thought was chocolate, and later after being rushed to the hospital, they learned that I had eaten four bars of laxatives that had been sent in the mail as samples. As an adult, I learned that this was not my first hospital scare, it was my second and would not be my last! The devil tried to kill me early in life.

As we continued, to travel and attend church. At one nightly prayer service, I was called out of the audience. The preacher that night talked about my life and told me that for the rest of my life that God had assigned Psalm 23 to me and that I needed to repeat it every day. If you don't know this scripture and have been following my story up until this point. Psalm 23 is a scripture that talks about God being our protector and provider. Understanding more now than I did when I was younger, I have come to realize that my imaginary friend was God. I know the part in Psalm 23 when it says The Lord is my Shepherd,

I shall not want… He fed me the morning that I was hungry at my best friend's house before school and when it says, Yeah though I walk through the valley of shadow of death that he is with me. He was always with me. All the days that I spent in my room crying, now I know that he was there. He went on to say that one day I would have enough money that I would be able to place bags of food on people's doorsteps.

Watching the change in my mother, I knew without a doubt that God was real. My mother had changed the way she dressed. She stopped playing cards, drinking, cursing, and never smoked another cigarette again. Everything about her seemed new.

Chapter 6

Not Me!

Every day seemed to be different now. I was developing in ways that I never knew would or could happen. I had started my period at nine but never knew what it was. It came and went away. Something was happening to me, and the only person that I told was my best friend. Although my mother's life was different, she was still very strict, and I was always afraid to disappoint her. I had officially started my period. When I shared this with my bestie, she told me that I had to tell my mother because I might bleed to death.

By this time, my mother's husband, my new stepfather, had retired and moved in. We had a happy home for once. My mother would cook breakfast and dinner. For lunch, I was pretty much on my own, but there was always a lot to choose from. My stepfather loved to go fishing. He would get up early in the morning and would always make sure that I had breakfast, a boiled egg, and toast. I would ask for coffee, but he would tell me that it would make me black. Wasn't I already black? I didn't know any better, so I stayed away from coffee because that must have been something terrible. He always looked out for me, which you will understand more throughout my story.

When I finally got the courage to tell my mother that I had started my period, the only thing she said to me was, "If you have sex, you will get pregnant." Sex? What does that entail, I wondered? I was only fourteen years old. She didn't talk to me about what a period meant, as it related to caring for myself, nor hygiene. I had to figure all these things out on my own. I recall one Sunday going to church with my best friend and having an accident in my clothes. It was a beautiful, violet corduroy ankle-length skirt, with a matching vest. Her mom took me in the bathroom and helped me clean up. I was so embarrassed. My self-esteem continued to dwindle. When I would look at myself, I never saw the smart, beautiful brown skin girl in the mirror. I saw a girl with a big forehead, buck teeth with a gap, and big lips. These are all the names that the kids would call me when they would pick on me at school and in the neighborhood. I felt like such an ugly duckling. They say that sticks and stones may break your bones, but words will never hurt you. This is a complete absolute lie! The reality is that those words did hurt me then and for many, many years to come. They slowly chip away at who I was purposed to be.

As my body continued to develop, I inherited traits from both my mother and my grandmother, where my breast was large for my age. I started to get the attention that I wasn't used too from the boys in the neighborhood. Before when they would play, hide and seek. I would try to figure out why I was the only one that would return to base, but now as I started to get more attention, I know that the hide and seek was really, find and fool around. I never thought much about the meaning of fooling around until later when I became the fool!

My freshman year in high school was off to a great start. I was still very academically inclined, an honor roll student, in the band, choir, and a cheerleader for the Beddingfield Bruins. Our colors were light blue and gold. I had gained a new set of friends that were in the same activities as me. Although my bestie and I were practically like sisters, we had different dreams and aspirations. As kids, we would play church, which was what we knew. One day I would be the Preacher, and she would be the choir. We took turns. As we got older, we both played basketball in middle school until one day, we both went for the ball at the same time. She came down on my head, and I bit a hole in my tongue. My father had started to visit more in my middle school days, coming to the basketball games and taking my friends and me out for pizza. All my friends loved when he would come into town, pulling up in whatever new Mercedes was out at that time. Everyone thought we were so well off because he would take everyone to the local Pizza Inn. The appearance of wealth was only for an outward show.

During my high school years, I dreamed of the day that I would leave Wilson, go to college, and return to the city. I wanted to live a corporate lifestyle and become a CEO with my own business. My bestie wanted to be married, with children have a beautiful home and get a good job. Therefore, we took different classes and started making new friends. Our relationship began to struggle from time to time, but I always looked at her as my dearest friend.

I met a young guy that was popular at school because he was recognized as one of the best football players on his middle school team. A lot of people knew him right away. He lived in phase two of our community. I lived in White Oak East, and he lived in White Oak West. They were walking distance from each other. He started hanging around our neighborhood more frequently. I knew his best friend because he was my first crush in middle school. When you are that young, was he a crush or boyfriend, I don't know. I am not sure what to call him, but we liked each other. This boy was very cunning and made me feel special. He would make me laugh and show up at my window late at night just to talk. We would also talk on the phone until we fell asleep, then wake up to each other the next morning. I felt so special but would soon learn that I wasn't the only one that he made feel special.

One night when my mother was deep in sleep, he showed up at my window with the most adorable puppy and convinced me to let him in. When I didn't get caught, this became more frequent. He came by every night with his charm and smile. Then, one night, I lost part of me. Something that I could never get back, ever again. It would change the course of my life forever.

He now called me his girlfriend, and we started to hang out more and more. His mother worked and was not home during the day, unlike my mother, who was a stay at home mom. Although he was kind to me, he started to get in trouble in school and started to get suspended often. What I didn't know is that when I wasn't with him at the house, someone else was. He was quite popular with all the neighborhood young girls. I wasn't the only one that lost herself. Later in life, I learned that many of my actual friends lost their virginity to him as well.

This popularity with other girls put me in a place where I started to be disliked. There was one girl that was older than me and more experienced. She turned one of my friends against me to the point where she started to bully me. I would be over his house, and they would show up. I was so naïve and had no idea what was really going on. I was intimidated by both girls. I started to skip school just to be able to spend more time with him, alone at home because I knew if he didn't get it from me, he was getting it from someone else. This only angered this girl more to the point where they would chase me in my car and follow me home.

One night, while I was downstairs watching tv. I heard yelling coming from outside of my house. When I went outside, there they were, the two neighborhood bullies. This girl was determined to get me away from this boy. My mother had been out on the porch while my bully yelled, "Come outside, you little bitch!" I went back downstairs to tell my stepfather, and he told me, "Listen, if you don't fight her, she will never leave you alone. Come here!" He took me in his storage closet and told me, "Put this padlock on your middle finger, ball your fist up and go out there and beat her ass!" At that point, I felt so empowered I ran outside, jumped off the porch, and started throwing blows as they would say. I was hitting her as hard as I could with my fist that had the padlock. What was I doing? All of this over a boy, really? I wasn't a fighter...

I had so many responsibilities during this time in my life that it caused me to have to grow up fast. Three years prior, my sister, that was born before me, the pretty one was murdered. She was found dead in an alley in DC as a result of a hate crime. Although she was said to be the prettiest out of all my mother's daughters, she identified as a man and would dress like one. She left behind two little boys who were now being raised as my little brothers. I took the oldest everywhere that I went, but he had started to tell my mother what was going on. This didn't help me at all as my new boyfriend had decided that he was going to become a drug dealer. My mother's greatest fear was in front of her now. The child that she wanted to protect. The child that she Got Out, was now dating someone like this.

If you remember, I explained that my mother had nearly killed her first husband and was no stranger to going to jail. Although she had given her life to Christ and stopped drinking and smoking. I watched the anger that she once demonstrated ignite in her again, this time like I've never seen before. She forbids me to see this boy. I was placed on punishment but would just sneak out of the house and come back in the morning.

One day on the way to school, with my bestie in the car, I convinced her to skip school, and we went over to his house. She was so much wiser than me because that would be the last time, she skipped school with me. Yes, he was a drug dealer, but he never offered me drugs of any kind. On the weekends, I wanted to see him so bad that I would drive to his hang out in the city. I didn't realize that this boy was doing something so criminal that he could go to jail and take me along with him. To this day, I still don't understand how I could have been so stupid. Yes, I just called myself stupid because I was doing crazy things. I'm sure the low self-esteem and self-worth had something to do with it. I had gotten close to another girl that was on the cheerleading squad with me. One day we picked him and his best friend up from what they called the block. A police officer followed me after picking him up and pulled us over then asked for my license and registration. I was a new driver, so I didn't have it handy and ended up dumping everything out of my purse, including the first bible that I had received when I was baptized.

The officer let us go that day. As I drove off, when we got further down the road, my boyfriend asked me to pull over. He got out of the car and began to shake his pants, little did I know, crack values started to fall out of his pants. This could have been the end of my life and I was too naïve to even know that. Now I am reminded of the promise made to me of Psalm 23 – The Lord is my shepherd. Sheep are dumb, and they often find themselves in places where the Shepherd must come and rescue them. I know that God saved me on this day, and it wouldn't be the last.

Soon after this happened, we broke up, not because of what happened with the police, it ended because I was tired of catching him with girl after girl. I would go to his house, and there would be another girl there. We would argue, and he would make it seem like she was his girlfriend. My, my... had the tables turned, now I was like the girl that had harassed and bullied me, but I finally understood why she was acting that way. He had done the same thing to her that he was now doing to me.

For the remainder of my freshman year, I refocused and went on about my life. In my sophomore year, one day after a carnival event that we were having at school, while in my cheerleading uniform. There was this guy that stood 6 feet tall, smiling at me. He played basketball at one of the local high schools and was so handsome. He looked nothing like my now ex-boyfriend who was height-challenged. I'm not sure what I saw in him, but when you have never felt love before and don't know what love is, you cling to what feels like love. He soon asked me out. I had never been asked out on a date before. I met him at his house. The date ended up being dinner with his family. I recall his mom not being nice to me. She threw money at me for dinner, then looked at him and said, "She is too young for you." My heart sank. I felt rejection, like how my mother had treated my ex. I wasn't good enough to date someone like him. She was right about the age he was a senior in high school, and I was a sophomore. He was much more experienced than me but tall, a star on the Fike High School basketball team, with a smile that could not be denied.

That didn't stop us from seeing each other. My mother approved of the relationship. When he knocked on my door to see me, I was startled and afraid that I was going to get in trouble. My mother did the unthinkable, she let him in and told me that I had a guest. This was unreal, this guy had shown up at our house unannounced, and my city mother let him in. You must understand that even though we were in the country, my mother wasn't the drop by our house type. I guess she approved of me seeing him because she could control the dating. We would sit in the living room and do our homework then he would attend church with us on Sundays. What my mother didn't know was when we left the church, that we would drive separately to take advantage of the time alone while she attended second and third service. We were alone, and spent this time having sex. He was worse than my ex because he was deceitfully cunning. He came like a sheep in wolves' clothing.

There was no way for me to know what he was doing from day to day because he went to Fike High School. One day, my mother asked him to go to the grocery store for her, and he took my car. This is important because while he was there, he met another young lady, and they exchanged numbers. I found out about their relationship about a week later. One Sunday, we had gone back to my house after church to have sex like normal. On the same day, my best friend let me know about the other girl. We got into a huge argument. When I was taking him home, I ended up putting him out of the car half-way to his house, and I returned home. When I got back, I started to have remorse and called his house. His mother, who still didn't like me, said that he had taken the car and gone to the mall to pay a bill for her.

The reason that she was so willing to tell me where he was going was that she knew about the other girl. I had gotten more details from my bestie about the girl, after dropping him off. Can you believe this, I knew her...? She sat behind me in Geometry class. She was older than me but clearly not as smart as me because she was a grade behind. I recall her asking me about him while we sat in class. I didn't think anything was wrong because everyone knew that I had been seeing him, but now it all made sense. She had been talking to him all along. The worse thing that you can do is ask another woman about her man while you are stealing him or, in this case, dating him.

My bestie and me got in my car and headed to the mall. On the way there, he pulled out of her neighborhood in his mother's car right in front of me, so I followed them. When he realized that I saw him, he started to drive faster, trying to lose me, but what he didn't know is that I knew where they were headed. When he arrived at the mall, I was right there waiting. When they pulled up in the car before I knew it, I jumped out in the spirit of my mother someone was going down that day! I immediately started punching her and grabbing her hair! Then he jumped in between us, so I turned and started smacking him but every time I could get a hand free; I hit her. The girl ran, found an unlocked car, got in, and locked the door.

Heartbroken, I fell back into the arms of my ex and immediately started having sex on a regular, it became part of what we did when we were together. For me, I felt loved, not knowing what love was about. My mother never told me that she loved me nor hugged me. She never even said daughter; you are beautiful. I looked for this

44

attention elsewhere. On this day, for no reason, he looked at me and said I think that you are pregnant. Pregnant? What do you mean?!... Yes, that's me, Miss Stupid! If you have sex, you will get pregnant. Isn't that what my mother told me when my period started. Did I think that I was untouchable? Yes, I was college-bound. Yes, I was an honor roll student. Yes, I was a cheerleader. Yes, I sang in the chorus. Girls like me don't get pregnant. No, not me, are you kidding me?

Chapter 7

Expecting

When the summer approached, I started working at McDonald's. I had completed my first year of high school. My relationship with my mother had fallen apart because I refused to stop talking to this boy. So, I took a different path and started to reach out to my father, more and more. I'm not sure why I did this, but I wanted to get back at my mother and what better way to feel like I was right than to get my father on my side, who didn't always agree with my mother.

My stepfather and I were close as he had been a stable part of my life since I was a baby. Growing up, when my mother would punish me, my stepfather would always say, "She's gone now, come out of that room." We would sit and watch WWF and cowboy movies, that was his thing! When we would hear my mother pull in the carport, I would return to my room like nothing ever happened. Even when I would have terrible cramps, balled up in a knot, and home from school, he would be the one trying to help me. I remember he would say, "Put a pillow under your back." He was a good father to me, but with the relationship between my mother and me being so bad, I felt like I wanted to leave. One night my mother said something about my ex that upset me, and still today, I cannot believe that I turned to my mother while walking up the stairs to my bedroom and said: "FUCK YOU!" She was more hurt than angry because she didn't kill me. I've wished every day of my life that I could take that back, I didn't mean it and remain remorseful like it was yesterday.

My father agreed to allow me to come up for the summer and visit. I quit my job at McDonald's after only three weeks. My mother hated the idea, but because we were always arguing, she allowed me to go. I was now back in Washington, DC and saw a side of my father that I hadn't seen before; it wasn't just about driving expensive cars and wearing the best suits.

My father loved the finer things in life. When I was thirteen, he took me to New York for the first time, and we shopped for four hours. As a child, he would teach me how to shop for unique items that other people would not wear. On this trip, he bought me a $400 pair of boots that I thought were the ugliest shoes that I had ever seen. Most people where I lived their mortgage wasn't $400. Talk about a terrible waste of money as I never wore them. Besides, I was only thirteen! He was still quite the womanizer. While we were in New York, my father was unable to find a parking space, and I recall him leaving his then-girlfriend in the car in the summer heat for four hours while we shopped.

Growing up, I always had the first of everything. When the Pepsi phase hit, I had all the new clothes. When the female rappers Salt and Pepper came out with their trending style, I had the customed leather bomber jacket with the black rider boots. As a city girl living in the country, I stood out exactly how my father wanted me too.

While staying with him, I realized why my father had stopped coming around. Things changed after that New York trip and when I turned thirteen. My grandfather no longer showed up on the last day of school to pick me up for the summer. My great summer escapes had stopped and created a distance for me in later years from my father's side of the family.

Could the number 13 be a bad luck number? This year was a traumatic year, not only for me but for my entire family, everything CHANGED! My stepfather had a stroke that left him paralyzed on one side. He was a heavy drinker and a diabetic who also had high blood pressure. I'm sure all the fried chicken, pork chops, and mac&cheese that my mother cooked weren't helping much either. My mother was overwhelmed. Her daughter murdered a year earlier, left her with two young boys, and now her husband was in the hospital. When he was released from the hospital, he needed more care than any of us. He needed to be bathed, and at thirteen, I was assigned to help with that. Geesh, can you imagine being thirteen and having to bath an almost sixty-year-old man? I don't ever want to relive those days again. My mother became so overwhelmed trying to take care of everyone that after a year or so, she stopped taking care of herself. She forgot to breathe! Until one day, it all came crashing down. She had a nervous breakdown and had to be admitted into the hospital.

By this time, my stepfather had learned to bathe himself and was walking with a cane. He suggested that instead of us going to a family member's house that we should stay home and that I could cook. I was doing laundry, frying chicken, and caring for my nephews, who I considered my little brothers. It was such a hard time for us; I recall one day; my oldest nephew or little brother had gone into the refrigerator and was eating raw sausage links. I was so scared and upset that I spanked him, but instead of him crying, I sat in the middle of the floor and cried. What I didn't know is that those tears would be a constant factor in my life. It was only the beginning; my life as a child was over.

My father had changed as well since the last time that I saw him. He didn't have the fancy cars nor the beautiful home; he was now living in an apartment in South East DC off Martin Luther King Blvd. If you know anything about DC, this wasn't the best area to live. He had multiple girlfriends staying there but at different times. It was like watching a revolving door as they came and went. I would walk to a nearby payphone during the day and call my boyfriend collect. One day after my father's girlfriend had cooked breakfast, I got sick and went to the bathroom where I released my entire breakfast. Later that day, she asked me if I was pregnant, and I immediately told her no. Not me, are you kidding… So, I started to be mean to her, telling her about all the other women that would come to the house when she left. Now I was creating a distance between my father and me. Why would I do that? I had become such an angry person on the inside. I was trying to avoid what everyone else seemed to know already. I hadn't seen my period for a few months now, and I should have known.

Soon, I called my oldest brother, who was now remarried and had a newborn little girl. He and his wife came to pick me up from my father's. My father told him that he thought that I was pregnant. For some reason, I felt comfortable being transparent with my brother's wife when she asked if I was. I told her that I didn't know. So, she took me to the clinic. When the results came back, yes, I was EXPECTING. The honor roll, college-bound, now country girl was pregnant. What am I going to do? We talked about options, but my brother's wife said that my brother, who was training to be a Pastor would never allow it. Little Miss Naïve, didn't know anything about the options that were out there. I didn't have those type of friends that had abortions or even found themselves in this situation. It was time for me to tell my mother, and her response was, "I knew you were going to ruin your life! Now you are pregnant by this no-good boy that I told you to stay away from! Now, you figure it out because you can't come back here!". At this point, I had nowhere to go. How could I had been so naïve? The day that I found out that I was pregnant, I cried nonstop. I remember the day like it was yesterday.

My brother's wife felt sorry for me, and they decided that I could stay there with them. I was three months pregnant. Over the summer, while they were at work, I stayed home and became their babysitter. His wife had also researched options for me to go to night school after the baby was born. My dreams of college seemed to be nonexistent now. I didn't see a way out, so I agreed. My father had nothing else to say to me after that. He never checked on me or asked if I needed anything.

During the summer, I started to resent my current situation. Although they were trying to help me, I started to dislike everyone. This was not supposed to be my life, no, not me! One of my friends reached out to me, who found out that I was pregnant from hearing it from other people. My mother was telling the entire town that I was pregnant and how I had ruined my life. That just made me even more bitter and embarrassed.

Chapter 8

The Whispers

When I returned to school, it was my junior year. I was always a good dresser, so I put a lot more into the first day than usual. I had on a black ruffled mini skirt that flared at the bottom and a loose-fitting top as I was trying to camouflage my stomach. The entire day I saw people whispering among themselves. Even my teachers were looking and pointing at me. I had to tell my cheerleading coach that I would not be returning. I could see the disappointment in her eyes. She just shook her head. During this time, teenage pregnancy was rare. I may have been one of the first ones in my high school that this happened too. Even one of my middle school teachers found out and told others how disappointed she was in me. I just hung my head low. My self-esteem just continued to get lower and lower. I was so ashamed that I spent more time home that year than in class. My mother would look at me and say, "Look how you have ruined your life, I knew you were going to be nothing"! She even told the few friends that I had left that they should find new friends and asked them why they would want to be around someone like me. Many of them listened, except for a few.

That was a rough nine months of my life. I cried every single day. The whispers… "Who do you think the father is, I hear it's the drug dealer guy…". "No, it's the guy that plays basketball at Fike…" I just wanted to escape it all and pretend that they were not talking about me. In life who we think we are, can be tainted by who others say that we are. This tainted view can change the course of your life and cause you to go in a direction that you would not have necessarily gone.

Remember the girl that I chased that jumped into an unlocked car, well she was also one of the whispers. She did everything she could to make me feel bad. Her and my ex Fike High School boyfriend were now in a full-fledged relationship, and she was wearing his class ring. My mother, as I learned much later in life, had gone over to his house to tell his mother that he had gotten her daughter pregnant. Given the fact that his mother didn't like me, I know that conversation didn't go well at all. Fike didn't matter to me, I knew who the father was. While I was in school, I got into an argument with another girl that was supposedly dating the boy from White Oak West, my first. That is what I prefer to call him at this point. There I was with a maternity sweater on yelling and screaming. Unknowingly, this baby had already been in a fight, was I going to put her through another one. Remember the day I jumped off the porch and was fighting before I went away for the summer? Have you figured it out? I was pregnant! One punch in the wrong place and the baby would have died.

Although I was no longer a cheerleader, I was still allowed to sing with the chorus, but when we traveled to other schools to perform, I had to sit on the side while they sang. Why would the school put me through this? For me, it was unavoidable since the chorus was an actual class. The only time that I didn't have to sit on the side was when the chorus director wanted to make an example out of me. During Christmas, he thought it was a good idea for me to sing a solo about Mary and her baby boy. My God, even as I write this, I can feel the hurt and pain that I experienced many decades ago. I was his burnt sacrifice; he made a mockery out of me. It didn't help that I was the talk of the town, even the gas station attendant knew. If the kids from my school weren't telling everyone, my mother was. I started to hate my life more and more. I didn't know anyone that this had happened too and had no one to talk to about it. Everyone, for the most part, stayed away from me, and I found a way to stay away too.

At this point, I wanted to disappear. I would do anything to miss school; most days, I would say that I wasn't feeling well just to be able to stay home. The school would send my work home. Eventually, I was called into the counselors' office and told that if I continued to miss school, I would not pass for that year. After that, I started to go to school, but I was so behind in Spanish class that I couldn't catch up. I had never in my course of attending school received a grade lower than a B. Now, my grades were less than average. I even received a D in one of my classes and was moved to another math class. I recall my algebra teacher tell me, "You don't know math at all" and recommended me for the remedial class.

Eight months pregnant now, I had purchased a crib and was in my room, putting the crib together alone. The interesting thing about this is that when I first returned home from the summer, my room was still filled with barbies and every collective item that you could think of. I had the most beautiful dollhouse with custom furniture. As I mentioned before, I always had things; I was just missing love. Soon after I returned home, my mother made sure to give my entire collection away to the little girl next door. She did this to hurt me and repay me for getting pregnant. Alone in my room again, a familiar place for me, I struggled to put the crib together. Finally, it was done! I learned quickly that I would be solely responsible for the care of my baby. I just didn't know what it all included.

Everyone tried to guess if I was having a girl or a boy. My mom decided to give me a baby shower. She was still a fantastic cook and was creative in preparing the food. There were pink deviled eggs, and blue cream cheese filled celery sticks. My favorite or craving at that time was carrot cake and pineapple. I would sit and eat it until I would get sick.

I finally had an ultrasound that showed the sex of the baby, and God had answered my prayers. I wanted a little girl, although everyone said you're going to have a boy. Although I hated the fact that I was pregnant, I wanted to have a say in it. In a moment of tears as they never seemed to stop flowing. I gave her to God. One day alone in my room. Yes, I started talking to my friend. I now knew that this wasn't an imaginary friend that I had been talking to since I was five; it was Jesus. Jesus was and still is my friend, my father, and my counselor, I gave my unborn baby girl to God. I remember saying, "God, I don't know what to do with a baby, so I give her to you."

Rough times continued in my home. My mother wasn't good at managing money, and with all the health bills from my stepfather, we would run out of money every month. Often my meals would consist of half-smokes and milk. I seldom had a full, balanced meal with fruits and vegetables. I wasn't hungry, but I wasn't eating the normal meal-plan of a pregnant woman.

In my ninth month, at my doctor's visit, she said that the baby would be born on January 31. My mother had decided based on the date, the father of my baby. In my heart, I knew, but my mother placed doubt in my mind; I had slept with both in the same month.

After breaking up with my mother's choice, I never dated him again. He would get so jealous that when I would meet White Oak West downtown on the block, he would tell my mother where I was, she would literally show up on the block and jump out Medea style… if you can imagine that! This happened before I knew I was pregnant, shortly before I would head to stay with my father.

On January 12, 1990, around 5:00 pm, my stepfather and I were having some words. That seemed to happen a lot now, I was so angry inside that I had turned against the very people that loved me. Have you ever heard the saying, "Hurt people, Hurt people?" Well, that was me. As I went to walk up the stairs, my stepfather said, "You better pack your suitcase!" I had a smart-mouthed response and said, "She's not due until the 31st", and at that moment, it felt like I had wet my pants. I went to my room, and it continued to happen a little at a time. I had no idea what was going on. I never had a Lamaze class or any discussion on what to expect during childbirth. I had gotten pregnant before taking a sex education class in school. I was very naïve. During the night, it happened even more. I got up in the middle of the night and put rollers in my hair just in case it was happening. I didn't want to be unprepared if I had to go to the hospital, I thought in my mind at least my hair would be done. This alone should tell you that I had absolutely no idea what I was facing.

The next morning, I went to my mother's room afraid and stood at her door. She was on the phone, and asked me if I was okay, I told her I could wait until she got off the phone. When she ended her call, and I told her what was happening. My mother panicked and asked, "When did it start, and was I feeling any pain?" She decided to rush me to the hospital. I just thought she was insane. She told me to get my suitcase and let's go.

There is a story behind the suitcase as well. It belonged to my grandmother. She had moved back to Washington DC when I was about eleven years old. When she would visit, she would always carry this small green suitcase, and on her last trip to my house, she gave it to me. At the doctor's office, the ultrasound said that my water had broken but not completely. I was checked into the hospital and placed in a room with another girl, who looked like she was on her death bed. She was in pain, but I felt absolutely nothing. Something else I didn't know was after my water broke, I wasn't allowed to eat anything other than ice chips and dum dum suckers. It would be a long day and night. When they examined me again, the doctor said she is not coming until tomorrow, which would have been January 14 and that they needed to induce me so that I wouldn't get an infection. Shortly after he left, someone decided that she didn't like that date and that the thirteen was a better date for her. Here we go again with the number thirteen. What a painful age that was for me, but they say out of your pain comes purpose. Could this be part of my purpose?

I soon began to experience pain that I had never felt before. My mother never left my side. Things happened in that room that I was not prepared for! No one prepped me for this experience! On staff were the nurse practitioner and two other nurses, all women. I heard my mother say, "Give her something for pain"! The longest needle that I've ever seen in my life was headed my way and soon injected in my back, but the pain continued. They gave me more.

I should have known this was going to be painful because this little girl was strong. I would often see her foot pressed against my stomach, and she kicked all the time. I used to say, "She's going to be a cheerleader one day!"

After the second shot or epidural, what was once pain now felt like tremendous pressure. It was a long delivery process and took nearly an entire day. Finally, it was time! I pushed, and my mother rubbed my head, and I pushed until finally, she had arrived. When she came out, she was white as snow, they tried to get me to hold her, but I was afraid. I thought something was wrong with her, then they told me to push again and out came the most disgusting blob. I started to scream! I thought I was having another baby and that it was dead. I was so traumatized. How could this be happening to me? It wasn't another baby; it was the placenta. Again, no one explained this to me.

When I woke up, my mother had already contacted the one that she chose and told him his daughter was born. I saw him walk pass the room. He never spoke to me but went to see the baby. I was never given the opportunity to make the decision on my daughter's father. In fear of my mother, I kept my mouth closed. My mother told me when I came home that if I chose to be with White Oak West, then I had to leave her house. Now I had someone else to worry about besides myself. I had brought another life into this world, and now what was I going to do.

Chapter 9

She is Here!

The little feet and fat thighs. Jet black curly hair and caramel skin. What a beautiful baby doll? Despite what everyone told me, she was a good baby. She slept most of the day and night. Everyone said that I would be up all night, but that never happened. My beautiful doll baby was named by her grandmother. Yes, in my heart of hearts, I knew who her father was. I had gone to White Oak West house one day before my gift was born to talk to his mother. I explained my situation, and she asked if I would give her the name. I agreed.

Two weeks after she was born, his mother and her friend arrived at my house. My mother wasn't home, and they both came in to see her. She looked at me and said, "This is my grandbaby." I responded, "No, ma'am." Three months later, White Oak West showed up at my house with his best friend. We sat in the living room as I held my beautiful doll baby. He looked at me and said she belongs to me. I had to tell him that she wasn't his. Later, I heard that he went home and cried. What he didn't know was that I cried too, in fear of not being able to care for my daughter.

The one that my mother chose could care less about her, but his mother seemed to fall in love. He would come and pick her up and take her to his mom's every week. When she left, I felt like part of me had left as well. She had brought a new life to the house. Even my stepfather was smiling again. He would hold and rock her in his recliner all day while I was in school. Yes, I went back to school one week after I had her. I had a new motivation for my life. Even the cafeteria lady looked at me and said, "There is something different about you." She had no idea I wasn't alone in this world now. I had a huge responsibility. This responsibility made me realized that I had to get my life together and gave me a renewed determination. I worked and studied harder. I had to focus hard to get caught up.

It was now the second half of my Junior year, and prom was right around the corner. I never thought that it was an option for me, so I didn't even try. My mother seemed to have a change of heart toward me now. It was as if she supported me again. It was different from how she treated me while I was pregnant. She found out about the prom from my best friend, who was planning to go and asked if I wanted to go. Of course, I did, but now I didn't have a date. Who would want to go to the prom with me? The girl that just had a baby. I was still ashamed of being a teenage mom. Why Not Me! Turned into a Yes Me!

While in history class, it turned out that one of the guys in my class and I were the only ones that didn't have a date, so we decided to go together. Things are looking up for me. Maybe my life isn't over after all. That night was exciting, especially getting out and not having to think about being a mother. I felt like I could be a teenager again. I had danced the night away, but it didn't end without drama. The girl that I was about to fight in the mall parking lot over the one who my mother chose decided that she wanted to flirt with my date. Clearly, she hadn't realized just how serious I was, but when I turned around and looked at her, she walked away. Tonight, wasn't the night, hadn't she already done enough. The rest of the night was excellent. When

I arrived home, my baby doll was sound asleep being rocked in the recliner by my stepfather. He was also in love. I felt like she gave him a purpose again. My mother was happy as well. Every day, she would put a different dress on her with matching shoes and a hair bow. It was as if she knew she had been given another chance. She seemed to brighten everyone's life day in and out. The house had laughter and love again.

It wasn't easy for me; I was still dealing with a lot of sadness and rejection. One day when the one my mother chose came to pick up my baby girl, he had another girl in the car. I was so hurt and angry. I could not believe that he would show up at my house to pick up my baby with another girl. Angry can't even describe how I felt; it was more like rage. My mother had never seen this side of me. I was cursing and yelling as loud as I could. All of which was a mask of how hurt and how alone I had started to feel. He would say things like, "Who do you think is going to want you now. No one wants to date someone like you". I shrank smaller and smaller, then to have him show up at my house with another girl. That meant that she was holding my precious baby. Later, instead of him bringing her back, his mother came back to drop her off, but she too had the girl in the car. This time, I didn't have to yell and scream because my mother had it covered. After they left, I went to my room and cried like I use to cry and just talked to God. I cried so often that it felt like there was a pain in my feet.

The summer approached, and I knew I had to get a job. My cousin was a maid in a downtown motel called the Heart of Wilson. I was thankful for her help but had no idea what I had just gotten myself in too. The summers in Wilson were hot, with temperatures reaching 100 on most days. The motel did not have an elevator and the laundry facility was across the street. I worked hard at everything that I did and would learn to work hard there, as well. Every day, I had to clean fourteen rooms and two townhouses. In addition to cleaning the rooms, we were required to wash, dry, and fold all the linen, towels, etc. that we used at the motel. The only good thing about my day at work was once you were able to get your cart loaded with the linen, towels and everything needed to clean the room, walking up and down two flights of stairs; you at least had a chance to enjoy the air conditioner from the hotel room. The laundry room was over 100 degrees at any given time because there was no air condition. I worked all summer, and I felt tortured every day. When the summer was over, I was able to buy clothes that I needed, pay for my senior pictures and a class ring. I also made up my mind that I had to find a way out. This type of labor was not for me!

I stopped thinking about college when I got pregnant. I no longer felt that it was an option for me. My daughter was growing fast, still bringing laughter back in the house. Every weekend she would get picked up and brought back. They never brought the girl to the house again, although I'm sure that she was still around. Whenever I needed anything for the baby, they would buy it and bring it, never giving money so that I could do it myself. It was a pretty bad situation to endure. The SAT was coming up, and I was scheduled to take it. I wasn't sure why I was taking this test as I was no longer college-bound; at least that was what I was thinking. I had a baby to take care of now. Nonetheless, I took the test, and later one of my dearest friends still today, who was determined that we were going to go to college, took it upon herself to apply for me to attend North Carolina Central University. When I was accepted, I figured that it was all a waste of time, but my mother said, "You are going to college, and I will keep the baby." Knowing what I know now, that was only partly good. It gave me an escape from my responsibility. I had just started to care for my daughter myself properly. My mother had been doing most of the work because I was in school all day.

My senior year in high school was a good year. I was nominated as part of the homecoming court. I had caught up in all my classes. I even had a boyfriend. He was different, almost normal compared to the other two guys. We had a sweet relationship. He wore my bomber jacket and one of my earrings in his ear. It was what they called puppy love. The year was moving fast; we had already taken our senior portraits and was preparing for graduation. I still didn't know what was next for me. I was called to the office one day to find out that my mother had already been contacted. The school was offering me a scholarship for nursing. I wasn't as excited as most would be because I still didn't think that college was an option for me until I learned that I had been accepted on the terms that I take the ACT exam. I had taken the SAT but wasn't serious about it because, in my mind, I thought that I wasn't going to go to college. I had started to settle with the idea that I would be in Wilson raising my daughter. It would be horrible; she was such a good baby.

After learning that college was an option, one weekend, my friends and I planned to spend the night together because the next day we were headed on our first college tour. Well, that was a night to remember, we ended up making a stop at a guy's house that one of the girls knew. There was drinking, but I didn't indulge, although one of my friends whose home we were staying at did. It didn't turn out well, and we didn't exactly know what to do other than hide it from her mom. We had to dress her the next day and drive to the college, which was about two hours away. She was in bad shape and looking back; we could have lost her to alcohol poisoning. I am so thankful to God that she was okay. The tour went well, and we had an opportunity to visit a cousin of mine from DC that was a star football player at A&T University. Although we had a good time, none of us decided to attend that college.

Here we are, finally! It's graduation day. This should have been the most exciting day of my life, but instead, it was filled with pain and grief. My grandmother, who was still living in Washington, DC, was rushed to the hospital, on my graduation day. My mother had to choose whether to see her first out of five children graduate from high school or see her dying mother. She realized that her mother was going to pass before she would arrive, so we headed to graduation. In all my pictures, you could see the joy and sadness in my mothers' eyes. I cried and cried that evening when they called my name, the girl next to me had to tell me to go! My daughter was born on my grandmother's birthday, and she was the only one she would want to hold her when she was around. I can understand that. My grandmother was a heavy lady and soft like a pillow. I recall laying on her arms when I was a little girl and trying to fluff them like a pillow while in church. I will forever miss her. My graduation day was like starting a new chapter and closing one at the same time.

My mother and my cousin attended my graduation. My father did not attend nor call. I had not seen or heard from him since the day that I left his house to go and stay with my brother. He had not even taken the time to come and visit his firstborn grandchild. Was it because he knew what my mother told me on my eighteenth birthday? My life had one twist and turn after the next, it was worse than a soap opera, and this was the worst twist yet! After picking out my senior prom dress, my mother told me that the man that I had known and loved as my father was not my father. Does this sound familiar? Why is this happening to me! This was some type of family norm; my grandmother did the same thing to her, and would I one day do the same thing to my daughter?

After graduation, we left the next day and headed to Washington, DC, so that my mother could begin to make funeral arrangements for my grandmother. We were out of town for a week. When I returned home, I went to see my boyfriend, and when I got to his house, there was another girl there. Here I go ago again, but this time, it was like a light turned off. The hurt felt like pain. I would never trust again. I demanded that he give me my jacket and earring back that he claimed he had lost. I could not believe that he had cheated on me, and I never talked to him again. It was probably for the best anyway. On prom night, he placed me in a terrible situation. After prom, he had gotten a hotel room with his friends. I had no intention of staying with him; he asked if I could wait there while they went to drop off the rental car, but he didn't return until about four hours later. I had no way to get in touch with him. I was terrified of calling my mother. She never believed anything that I would tell her. So, I waited and waited. While I was waiting, the phone rang. I thought it was him, but it was my mother. She didn't allow me to explain; she yelled and told me that I had to leave her house. I was in tears. I had spent my entire senior year trying to get my life back on track, and this happens. When he finally arrived, he was so intoxicated that his friends merely dropped him off at the room. He wasn't even able to stand up, and I had no one to call. When I made it home the next day, sure enough, my mother had trash bags on the porch with my clothes. I had to beg and plead for her to listen to me and to believe me. She never did but allowed me to stay.

I had come to a point in my life where I wanted out, and I believed college was my exit plan. I had an opportunity to leave Wilson, something that I always wanted to do. I was headed to college, but what about my sweet baby, you might ask? Well, she was primarily being taken care of by my mother and stepfather. Also, my two nephews or brothers, which is how we were raised, kept her fully occupied. I had a car, and the plan was to come home on the weekends. If I had to do it all over again, I would have taken her with me and figured out how to make it work.

Chapter 10

Escaping

It was time to head to college. It wouldn't be unfamiliar to me because I had the opportunity of attending a summer pre-entry program, and I am glad that I did. I made a lot of friends and learned my way around the campus. I also bonded with a guy from Portsmouth, Virginia, who became smitten with me. We forged a friendship and talked to each other every day after the program until it was time to start classes. For some reason, I didn't feel the same way about him and viewed him as a friend to me. He was handsome and very charming, but there was something that kept me from falling for him. He would bring me roses and buy me gifts. I knew that he liked me, but I was not ready to offer him more.

The day that the man that I thought was my father dropped me off at college was oh so real. Was this happening? Have I been given the opportunity for a better life, I thought? Right before he left, I was expecting a father, daughter speech. College was very familiar to him and his family. He and his siblings had all been college graduates. Instead of the father-daughter talk that I was hoping for, he said there is something that I need to give you and handed me a brown paper bag. When I opened the bag, inside was a box of condoms with no explanation. He was the man that for 15 years of my life, I had dearly referred to as Dadly. The man that taught me about fine dining and how to dress had practically no farewell pardons for who he believed to be his firstborn child, his daughter. Surely, he was happy that I was doing something with my life. I hadn't gotten trapped in the mantra of being a pregnant teen who dropped out of school to do nothing with her life. I pressed forward and was the first to finish high school and the first to attend college out of my siblings. My mind was racing; he had nothing to say, nothing! Was this what our relationship had dwindled too? I was sure this would be a proud bonding moment, but it wasn't. I took the bag and said thank you. Then I went on with my life. My freshman year seemed like a fresh start. Where no one knew anything about me, the person that I had become to others; I left behind in Wilson. I never disclosed to anyone that I had a daughter; it was as if it never happened. College life was my first time being on my own without adult supervision, and I enjoyed every minute of it. I remember less about my classes and more about them on and off-campus parties. We had a place on campus called the sweatbox. All the newbies or freshman would hang out there every week. When we weren't hanging out there, we were hanging out on the yard.

My classes were somewhat easy except I was having challenges with my English Literature course and found myself in the library, frequently. While studying one day I notice a young man that was in my class. Curious, I wanted to know if he was having similar struggles and he indicated that he was doing well. In addition to needing help, he became my new friend, hanging partner from the malls to the cheap lunch spots. Listen, we were hungry college students. Dating was never a thought as I was not his type as he would say. Nevertheless, this young man has remained one of my closest friends even until today. He is reliable, trustworthy, supportive and became an uncle to Baby Girl.

Eagleson was my dorm, and there I was a freshman or Freshmeat as they called it. One evening after coming back from the cafeteria, a few guys were hanging out in front of the dorm. I stopped to talk to one of them, and before I knew it, we were meeting on a regular. It was not a relationship, although at that time I thought that it was. I knew nothing about a freshman being Freshmeat. I just saw a tall, handsome guy that was interested in me and that knew nothing about me. Maybe he will love me. Most nights, we would have sex in his car. I don't ever recall him taking me out on a date or doing anything nice for me. For a matter of fact, I was the one doing things for him. After I went to college, I obtained a college benefit from the man whose last name I carried as my father. I started to receive a check for $400 per month from the military. That was a lot of money back then, and my college boyfriend did not hesitate to ask. I recall the first thing he asked, was could I help him get some tires on his car. I fell for him hard, of course. He was an upperclassman and popular because he played basketball. Does this sound familiar? Here I go again, and you would think that I learned my lesson. I wanted him to like me so much that I would just have sex with him in the car on dead-end streets, or wherever we could park.

My University was a HBCU, and on campus, there were fraternities and sororities. I started to get mean looks from one of the sororities and later found out that it was because of the guy that I had been seeing. The reason we were having sex in the car and never going on dates was that he had a girlfriend. She had recently graduated, and I learned that the relationship was serious. Then the arguments started, and yes, he denied it. The denial wouldn't last very long because I stopped agreeing to meet up with him and soon found out that they had moved in together. That didn't seem to stop him; he would invite me over. I went over once, but I was hurting on the inside. I remember him telling me when I was at their apartment, how he had bought her some jeans and she didn't like them. I'm standing there getting dressed and

69

feeling like a complete fool. I'm not sure why I continued to allow this to happen. After that day, I was determined to move on, although we continued to talk on the phone, until the night before he got married. Yes, I said, married. Can you believe he is getting married? Well, I couldn't either because he was on my phone crying and asking me to please come and see him. I'm sure you already know, yes! I went to see him. The night before he was going to marry someone else, I was there. We were having sex, and the door opened.

Being on campus and away from home, I had escaped the bad reputation that I had earned. Now I was on new territory enjoying the 10:40 break, jamming to 90's hits, while hanging out on the yard, watching the fraternity or sororities stroll showing off their new pledgies or steps. If you were a freshman, this was an hour that you did not schedule classes; it was a must to be on the yard. It was the time to shine in your best new gear, and your lip gloss had to be popping. It was also the time to see who the next hot attraction was. I started to get the attention of a few guys at this point. One was known for his style; he would wear the matching hat, shoes, jacket, and belt. He was from Connecticut, and his style was different. He was very flirty but polite and had an amazing smile. I'm starting to see a trend here; I believe that I have a thing with smiles. It was hard to resist, but I didn't talk to him right away. I was trying to get over the hurt that I had just gone through.

Yes, me and Mr. Freshmeat had gotten caught but his soon to be wife would never know because the person that walked in the room was his best man. He only closed the door and never said a word. When I saw him again, he never made mention that he knew it was me and that I was even there. After that night, I knew it was over for real this time, and it was farewell to my freshman love affair.

Time was moving so fast that I seldom went home. I would go back just enough that my daughter knew who I was but not enough to take on any responsibility. One weekend my mother demanded that I come home, and I told her that I wasn't feeling well because I wanted to attend homecoming at a local HBCU. Unfortunately for me, I had a car full of my friends all dressed up and while sitting in traffic. All we could hear was the squealing of tires, but that wasn't all, ambulances, police, and fire trucks were everywhere. Thank goodness we all walked away without a scratch. I believe that my mother knew that I was lying and was praying for me. A drunk driver hit me from behind while I was stopped in traffic, driving 60 miles per hour. It was no way we should have walked away, especially those in the back seat. The back of my car was so mashed in that the gas cap was hanging out. We were protected on that night and never made it to the party. Also, all my friends ended up suing me, but thankfully my car insurance paid them; unfortunately, it changed the dynamics of our friendship. My trust in relationships was getting even more tarnished.

It didn't take me long to bounce back; I was now dating someone new. Mr. Connecticut had won me over with his smile, and we spent a lot of time together. For once in my life, it didn't seem like it was only about sex. We still had sex a lot, but he would buy me beautiful things. He bought me an entirely new wardrobe. It seemed that he was at my place every night. Yes, time sure does fly. I was now in my sophomore year and had moved off campus. I had purchased another car that looked old and beat up when my mother and I found it for $3000. It was a white Porsche 924, 5 speed with a sunroof and black leather sport seats. I didn't know how to drive a stick shift, so I had to have someone drive me home.

My stepfather, although still paralyzed on his left side from the stroke, taught me how to drive the car while sitting in the passengers' seat. He was kind to me, better than the man that I was raised to believe was my father. I guess I can't expect, but so much, at least he moved me to college, which ended up being a disappointing day with him. I hadn't seen him since I left his house pregnant, and now I have a daughter that he has never laid eyes on. In all the fury of getting me moved out, I don't think he even greeted her, hugged her, nor introduced himself. That had to be very hard to do as she was the light in everyone's eyes, so full of energy with her own independence. This little angel was an old soul in a 1-year-old body. Unlike most babies, she never sucked a pacifier, and she slept all through the night, and at 1 ½ year old, she was already potty trained. It didn't take much. I would take her in the bathroom and show her how to use her little pot. It was quite unreal how she picked up on this. We would always go together making frequent trips, she would use her pot, and I would use the adult-only pot, which is what we told her. I didn't want her falling in! Until one day, she came to me and said, "Mommy, I went to the pot." I was shocked literally. I asked her, "Did you do 1 or 2, she answered and said 1 mommy and smiled with the biggest smile ever". Everyone in the neighborhood knew and loved her. She loved to be called by the nickname that my mother had given her when she was born. So, everyone would just say, "Hi Peaches!" She would walk around smiling and was still dressed in fluffy little dresses with bobby socks every day. I think my mother was going back in time and wishing that she still had a little girl and not one that was all grown up now.

My freshman year in college flew by, I did okay in my classes but could have been more focused. I tried to reintroduce myself to being a cheerleader, but that didn't work out for me, and I soon just did what most under-driven students did, hang out on the yard after classes. This year had exciting new loves, heartbreaks, and flings. In between my first college heartbreak, until I met Mr. Grey Eyes, there were many others whose names I can't remember. A few stood out, a Kappa who made me laugh, and it seemed that we talked all the time. I believed that he cared about me until I learned that he had a girlfriend at another college. He wasn't the only one; I was also dating Mr. Grey eyes, who wanted to be a Kappa. His standards were high; when I walked with him, I had to give off a very confident persona. I enjoyed my time with him. He would rub me down with Victoria's Secret lotion at night and light candles. I laugh inside as I write this thinking was that all that it took. A country/city girl searching for love, wasn't hard to please and during this time felt that this was the best anyone has ever treated me. I even recall us leaving his place one morning heading to class and had been chewing gum. I spit the gum out, and he almost had a fit. He said, "Don't you ever do that when you are with me again." When we were together, I always had to be on my best behavior. I remember my mother would say, "Stop frowning, you are going to get wrinkles, sit up straight with your shoulders back, cross your legs." The memories I will never forget, but he was also a fling and guess what, he had a girlfriend. Was this a perpetual trap? Would I ever break free from going around and around in circles?

My new roommate and I decided after the first semester of our sophomore year that we would move off-campus. At the time, this seemed like a good idea, but we had so much to learn. Would moving off-campus help us or pull us further away from our studies? Now, there were no rules nor dorm curfews, which didn't matter because we didn't follow them anyway. We had fun and new experiences in our place. I was still having flings, and she had her measure as well. We were alike in some ways and very different in others.

Nonetheless, we grew to be like sisters. I met a new guy when we moved to our first apartment that I did not consider a fling. I was determined to make him my boyfriend, but this came with its own set of issues. I spent a lot of time at his house and had a new experience with him sexually that kept me going back. I had my first organism. Can you believe that I'm disclosing ALL of this? YES, I am because I want to be FREE, and I firmly believe that some young, lost woman is going to read this one day. Hopefully, she will learn from my experiences and don't repeat the same mistakes. Speaking of orgasm, unfortunately, this wasn't my first time at the rodeo, but I was certainly late to the finish line!

You think your first time will be something magical, and for me, my response was, "Is that it?" You believe that you are missing out on something that you're late to the party. Everyone is talking about it, and you feel left out. Yes, out of all the men that I had been with already, I finally finished. Men finish all the time, and I had never finished. Young ladies don't let this happen to you. Psalm 139 tells us that we are fearfully and wonderfully made. You do not have to allow some man to make you a dumping ground!

This guy was an upperclassman who I enjoyed spending time with but would end in another heartbreak. I found out that he had a girlfriend back home. Since she was not there with us, I didn't let that stop me. I figured, why would he want to be with her. Surely, I was a better choice. Until one day she showed up at the house. This was a setup from another girl from his hometown. She didn't like my roommate or me and was determined to expose this relationship. What do you think happened? Well, there was an argument of course and guess what, he asked me to leave! My heart grew dark after that. I was determined not to care for anyone ever again.

While in school, to make extra money, I started to do girls' hair that was on and off-campus. Being off campus left me unexposed to the realities of college life. I grew further and further away from the relationships that I had once established. I even wanted to pledge into one of the Greek sororities, and I thought that I would be accepted with no problem. I had done some of the girls' hair at no charge. I guess that is what they consider hazing. Well, I applied and waited. The night before, while the decisions were being made, I received a call from one of my friends. She indicated that they had thrown her package in the trash. Since I did not doubt that I would be selected, I made a call, and her application was placed back in the process. On the day of selection, although they told us to come alone, we all went over in a group. The girls opened their letters and were all excited. I opened my letter, and it was a rejection. So much so that I started to feel lost, out of place, and shut down. I stopped speaking to all the girls that I once called my friends. Angry and bitter, I don't recall any of them reaching out to see if I was okay. My Kappa love reached out; he seemed genuinely concerned and promised that he would find out what happened. He had dated a couple of the ladies in that sorority at the time. When he called me back, I learned that one of my letters of reference did not recommend me for the sisterhood. As I think back, after almost 25 years, one of my referrals had asked me to volunteer at my former high school, and she would give me a letter. Well, I volunteered one day and never returned. I guess I thought she would give me a letter of reference anyway. If it were me, I wouldn't have written a good recommendation either. I should have kept my word and held myself to a higher standard.

Nonetheless, I didn't. I am also clear that I had chosen the wrong sorority because when I told my old dorm Resident Assistant, she indicated that she put my name in the box for her organization, which was the first of the divine 9. Looking back, I know that I made the wrong decision, I was looking for what was popular, and I dismissed what was real. I had a true big sister in her, a relationship that would never go away if I could only see then what I see now.

While doing hair, I met a lot of young ladies. One of which I became close friends with. I was introduced to an entirely different world of parties after we became friends. She was not in college. These were parties on a different level. She was older than me and a lot more mature than I had ever been. She had two beautiful little girls, and her mother was always there to help. She also had a boyfriend that had his own business; it just wasn't a legal business. But when she went shopping, she would say let's go! She often visited, and our first apartment became a popular hangout.

My roommate and I stayed in that apartment for almost a year, until one day after coming home from class, I found the door kicked in. We had been robbed! We immediately found a new place in the popular college community called Duke Manor. Most of the students who moved off-campus chose this apartment community, unlike our first place that was off the beaten path. We learned the hard way that we should have made a better choice.

Living off-campus separated me from the campus-life and 10:40 breaks. I went to class and left the yard after that because I was ashamed after being rejected. I did finally give into to Mr. Connecticut, but my heart was no longer warm. My new mentality was what are you going to do for me. I never expected to feel love again, but he eventually broke me down. He was spending most days and nights at my house, and for the first time, I experience a man doing something for me. Being as suave as he was, he decided that it was time for some new clothes, so he upgraded me with a new wardrobe. He purchased me a new television, and when Christmas came around because I shared the struggles back at home, he also purchased gifts for my two little brothers/nephews. I felt comfortable sharing with him; he was attentive and had a loving smile. I didn't feel disrespected in the beginning, but later, things changed. I am not sure what happened. I remember so vividly on Valentine's Day that he bought me the most beautiful red roses. Valentine's Day was unchartered territory for me; I had never had a Valentine nor anyone that cared enough about me to make me their sweetheart. So, I didn't buy him a gift. Not even a card, and he wasn't happy about it. As a matter of fact, after we had sex, he wanted me to leave. After that day, he started to treat me very dismissive. He loved to entertain and would have get-togethers at his house. When I would arrive, it was as if I didn't belong there. Other girls were hanging around, and he made sure that no one knew we were or had ever been an item. I was now a has been with him. One day I was at his house, one street over from our college campus. When, to my surprise, my car tires were slashed. Was I dealing with a jealous female, or was this get back from the girl whose car tires I had cut my freshman year? I would never know for sure. What I did know is that the fun ride with Mr. Connecticut had ended.

I was convinced now that I would just be by myself. The summer was approaching, and instead of going home, I stayed local, and my roommate and I decided to allow others that we knew to stay at our place while they were taking summer classes. The summer was a blur; I just remember being so broken-hearted, I had fallen in love with him. I also hadn't made it easy on him either. He was the next person that I had allowed myself to love, outside of Freshmeat. I cried and moped around for most of the summer. My friend that was staying with us at the time would try to encourage me.

Duke Manor had its own off-campus excitement. Since there were so many students living there, it was like a 10:40 off-campus break every day. There was a guy that saw me one day hanging off the building balcony as the guys would ride by in their cars. After he saw me, he never stopped riding by. He would call my name from outside of the apartment if he didn't see me. I was playing hard to get mainly because I just wasn't up to dating anyone at that time. One day when my new friend was over, I was telling her about this guy, it was crazy because I found out that he was her brother. Talk about a small world.

Chapter 11

Trapped

I was entangled in a world of parties, alcohol, and drug dealers. What had my life become? I was partying most of the time now as I had new local friends that did not attend college. My roommate and I spent most of our time modeling for hair shows now and hanging out. She worked a lot, so truthfully, I did most of the hanging out. I had started to date my friend's brother. Talk about a wild rollercoaster ride. I was partying and going to class. I made it to my junior year in college and was taking my nursing clinicals at Duke Medical Hospital. The clinicals consisted of me going onsite to the hospital and attending to patients. After being heartbroken, I had refocused on my schoolwork and was doing pretty good. I had excelled in a class that required an oral head to toe physical exam. This exam was a demonstration of knowledge that was completed in front of our professor. It was difficult, but I did well, most of the students did not receive a passing grade their first time around.

Partying and trying to go to class the next day was not mixing well. I soon started to miss class consistently. I also found myself drinking more and more, sex on the beach was my go-to drink. My new boyfriend was aggressive towards me and never took no for an answer. We began to fight regularly an afterward we had make-up sex. I didn't trust him because I would always catch him with other girls, but he kept coming back to me. I would check his beeper and write the numbers down. One night he didn't come to the house. He never let me spend a night alone. No matter what he was there, it would be very late; usually, at 4 am, but he didn't miss a night.

Being broken-hearted had increased my lack of trust. My insecurity had reached new levels. This time I got on my knees to pray. I hadn't prayed nor gone to church since going to college. It was almost as if I had forgotten about Jesus and how we would talk as I was growing up. I had a relationship with him that I had put to the side. On this night, I was reminded of God's love. I got on my knees and cried like a baby, and recall my chest hurting and my feet aching. I had so much pent-up emotional pain. What was it about him that was different from ALL the others? We fought all the time. I even recall the day I questioned him about another girl in front of his sister that I knew he was sleeping with, and for the first time in my life, a man hit me. He struck me so hard that he knocked me over the couch. The pain wasn't much, but the feeling of that happening to me hurt more. His sister was like you need to leave him alone. She had similar battles, and I had never met someone as strong as her. The father of her children was a kingpin drug dealer. These guys were different from what I had experienced with my daughters' father; this was on a level that I hadn't seen before. Did you catch what I just said, a kingpin drug dealer? I was in a domestic violence situation and dating someone that was on a kingpin level for dealing and trafficking drugs.

My life was different; I no longer had to hide who I was. I could be free to talk about my baby girl. Everyone now knew that I had a daughter. I even went home more, and every time I would leave, she would stand at the door and watch me leave holding Simba, her stuffed animal from the Lion King. Things had changed drastically in our home. My stepfather, who I loved as if he was my biological father, had passed away after being in a nursing home for a year. This happened towards the end of my sophomore year. His health had declined, and my mother was no longer able to care for him the way that he needed it. He hated her for putting him in a nursing home and treated her, so mean when she would visit. I would visit when I came home, and we would sit and talk. I could tell him things that I couldn't share with my mother. He would always say take care of yourself now and be careful out there! After his passing, at the funeral, my mother saw another woman there weeping and realized that she had seen her once before. My stepfather would always leave the house early every Saturday morning when I was about ten years old and take me with him. One day after we returned home, I told my mother about this woman's house that we would go to every weekend. My mother, of course, new right away and asked me if I could show her how to get there. That day I saw my mother was hysterical. The words no child should hear! After leaving the house and returning home, it wasn't over. I listened to my stepfather say okay I will end it. As the years went by, I was never invited out for a Saturday morning ride again. He would make me my boiled egg and take his fishing poles and leave. My mother realized at the funeral that he had not ended the relationship and learned that he never stopped seeing this woman.

A year after his death, my mother had slipped into a deep depression. She was no longer able to care for the boys, and they were getting into all sorts of trouble in school and the neighborhood. The oldest one was closet to me, and I could understand why she could no longer handle him. I had allowed him to visit with me over the summer, and he had taken my car one day while I was in class and was driving it around with no license or permit, he was too young for either. Then I found out that he had gone to the local store and bought cigarettes. This young kid was into everything. He was only twelve years old. So, I could understand why she couldn't handle him anymore. My oldest brother and his wife had taken them both into their home. They had relocated from Ft. Washington, Maryland to Clinton, Maryland.

When I would return home, I saw that my baby girl was not well taken care of. Her hair was not combed, and I could tell that she hadn't had a bath. I would tell my mother that it was time for her to come live with me, but she would say, "No, you are not taking her!"

As the year went on, the relationship with my friends' brother got more and more violent. We would break up and get back together. See God had not forsaken me, the night that he didn't come to the house, I prayed, and when I went back to bed, I had a dream, and in the dream, there were two women. One woman told me that she was his girlfriend and was asking me, "Who are you?" The other girl told me yes, she knew him, and they had been hanging out. The dream happened within an hour. If I had only gotten out of the relationship, then but I was trapped. I was trapped in my mind, trapped in my emotions, and held hostage to my own will because I didn't want to let him go. He had become my drug. One week after I had that dream, while I was at the house, he called and asked if he could put a car in my name.

The crew was on the way to buy new vehicles, something they often did because they had money to blow! I told him, no, and he wasn't happy at all. After he hung up, I changed my mind and called the number back, and I got a voicemail with a girl's voice. Her voice wasn't unfamiliar; I had heard it before. When I would check the numbers in his beeper, I had called a few of them previously, and I recalled the same voice. So, I waited for about an hour and called back. This time she answered the phone. I asked if this was his mother, and she said no and asked, "Who is this," I responded with "This is his girlfriend." Do you know what happens next? Well, she replied, "That is interesting because I'm his girlfriend." We ended up talking for over an hour. I learned that she worked at night, so while she was at work, he was at my house, and when I would leave out at 6 am to go to my nursing clinical, he would leave after me and beat her home. When she would get home, he would be there waiting. Since I wouldn't put the car in my name, he put the car in her name. She had been dating him since she was 16 years old. My immediate thoughts were, did his sister know? I considered her a good friend; then I remembered the day after I had the dream, I shared it with her, and now I understand the look that was on her face. She would just tell me to leave him alone. That was her brother, she wasn't going to share his personal business with me, but she would say to me, again and again, to leave him alone. If I had only listened, but I didn't. I could not mentally get away from this man; I was trapped. I continued to see him, and now the girlfriend had figured out where I lived and showed up to the house one night.

Chapter 12

Rejected

The way that Duke Manor was built, the bedrooms faced the outside breezeways that were like walkthrough balconies. We heard this loud bang on my bedroom window at about 2 in the morning, and he ran out. I listened to her scream, and that is when I realized that it wasn't just me, she was being abused as well. He left that night, and I didn't see him for a while. One night I decided to invite another guy over to the house. I had taken the drug dealers keys back, so I wasn't worried about him showing up. Little did I know that wouldn't stop him. While I had company, he showed up to the house. I ask my roommate if the guy could hide out in her room while I stood in the living room area where my drug begged for forgiveness and to give him another chance. He swore that he had ended the relationship and that I was the one that he loved. Yes, he would tell me he loved me all the time. He was the only one that had ever used the words; I love you. When we weren't fighting, he was always very passionate to me. He would make sure that I had the things that I needed and that my hair was always done. I had gotten used to the fast life and money. My roommate, unfortunately for me, got tired of having this guy in the room and put him out. When he came out of the room, he immediately started saying, "Man, look, she invited me over here, I didn't know that you were dating." As soon as he walked out of the door, the drug dealer had both hands around my neck until he had lifted me off the floor. He choked me until my roommate came out and started screaming stop! When he stopped, I fell to the floor, he then went to my room and loaded his gun with bullets that he had left there. The next thing I knew was that he had gone after the guy. We heard gunshots, and I was terrified. What had I gotten myself into? Soon he was back in my life and at my house every day. It was as if he was making sure that no one else had the opportunity to be with me, and I was too afraid to say no. One day I got a call from one of my friends that still lived on campus, and she told me that she had just seen him with another girl on the yard. I was reminded of my dream and went to look at the list of numbers that I had written down out of his beeper over six months ago. I called the on-campus number and ask for the girl by name who my friend told me she had just seen him talking too. This was the second girl in my dream. God had sent me a message. This girl explained that she had been seeing him for some time now. He was taking her to a hotel that was down the street from my house. I knew exactly where the hotel was as he had taken me there one night as a gift to me. The room had mirrors on the ceiling and a hot tub. In my mind, I thought that I was living my best life, but in reality, I was headed for destruction. I was afraid to ask him about the girl, so I never did. I just started to distance myself and not be available when he would page me. Yes, I had a beeper now too. When he was staying there, he would often leave things at the house and ask me to bring him something from time to time. One day I found my say weighing cocaine on a scale and taking it to him. God was watching over me even in my weaknesses. I never did drugs, but now I had gotten myself deeply involved.

During this time, the guy that had given me my first orgasm had called and asked if he could take me out. I felt that this was my way out of this relationship, and I said yes. We never made it out on the date; he didn't call nor show up. A few days had gone by when I found out why. He was dead! I was in shock and couldn't believe it. He had promised that he would be there to pick me up after he finished playing basketball with some friends. Well, he had a heart attack on the basketball court and died.

After catching my drug and being tired of the abuse, we were no longer on good terms. Instead of just walking away, I became the violent one and would find out where my drug was and caused arguments. I was approached by an undercover agent that wanted me to set him and the crew up, but no matter how upset and disappointed I was, I just wasn't built that way. I was too scared of him anyway; he would kill me. I would do nonconfrontational passive-aggressive things to hurt him and his longtime girlfriend. Once I called and had their electricity turned off in their apartment after finding out that they were living together. Later I reported that they were selling drugs out of the house and that there was always loud partying as if I was an angry neighbor. I knew that it wasn't true, but I pretended and complained until they were evicted from the apartment. We now had this love-hate relationship going on. I would do stupid things knowing that he would just come and be with me, and I didn't care even it was for just a moment. One day after having sex and an argument that made me finally wake up and realize that it was over, I left the house about an hour after him and was on my way home. I called my mother crying, and she said baby come home. While on my way home, on the side of the road, I saw him with the other girl from on campus. He was leaned up against her on her car; I blew the horn so that they both knew that I saw them and kept going. I had to get away from this guy. I had gone to have a yearly exam and received some not so good results. I had to get away from this man; my life was crashing before my eyes. I had to get home to my mother. Thank God it was curable but the embarrassment I could not hide. Did it take this for me to walk away? I had many reasons that should have caused me to walk away; him putting his hands on me and raping me when I refused to have sex with him should have been enough. Was I finally free in my mind to move on? If I kept messing with this guy, I'm going to end up dead one way or the other. Besides, this was a time when AIDS was finally being recognized. In my clinical at Duke Hospital, they would say that we were on the death floor because people were dying there. I had to watch them prep a young woman who had died from AIDS. A beautiful fair-skinned young woman that could have been about my age, now I realize that could have been me.

When I got home, I cried for a few days, and when I finally stopped, I realized just how bad things had gotten for my mother. The lady across the street from my mother called and said that she had been making sandwiches for my daughter to ensure that she had food to eat, but she needed more than that. My baby girl, although still smiling from ear to ear, was unbathed, her hair uncombed, holding on to Simba was now possibly going without food. I couldn't stand to think that I was so self-absorbed that I could do this to her. This time, despite what my mother had to say, I took baby girl with me, back to school with only the clothes that she had on her back. Now with baby girl with me, I knew that there would be no more him and me. No more fake trips where I thought he was taking me away when he was trafficking kilos with me in the car.

Chapter 13

God's Got Us

I woke up to reality; I woke up to my responsibilities. Despite my mother, it was time for me to be a mother to my daughter, and I didn't care what anyone had to say. When I returned to school, the first thing that I had to do was go and speak to the dean of the nursing program, which resulted in me having to go before the board of nurses for the program. I told them that I had not been going to class because of my mother's mental illness and needed to withdraw from the program. They were disappointed, but I knew that I had to do something to get my life back on track. I needed some time to get myself together, being that my daughter was now with me. No, I didn't drop out I just took a couple of months from that semester to get a job and figure out what was next for me.

I didn't discuss this new living situation with my roommate, and she was not happy, to say the least. It drove a wedge between us because she would always say that she didn't like children. My baby girl would be sitting at the kitchen counter, and my roommate would come in and not speak to her. Everyone loved baby girl, the smile and her cheeks were just undeniable. My roommate was determined not to be won over. Slowly our friendship and sisterhood was being destroyed. I never thought to ask her first; I felt that surely, she would understand. My other friend, even though I had finally stopped dealing with her brother, remained friends. We would hang out, and her mom would babysit all the girls. We still had some good times. I cared less about having a relationship during this time and more about getting a job and providing for my baby girl. It was a lot that I needed to teach her about just being a little girl. I was determined to make a good life for her. She never deserved me not being part of her life, but it wasn't easy.

I was able to change my major and return to school, thank God! I changed my major to Political Science with a minor in Public Administration. Everyone that cared about me that I had met at school supported me. I worked and took my baby girl to class with me when I didn't have a baby sister. The transition wasn't smooth. My friend's brother also found out where I was working and showed up at my job. The manager saw how afraid I was of him and asked if she should call the police after he came in and said, "Bitch, you see me come here! You know I will take care of you, why are you up in here?" I ignored him, but it was evident that I was afraid. I declined her offer to call the police and was determined to make it on my own. This job was horrible and, in a crime-ridden area of the city. Once, someone went into the dressing room and defecated. I was screaming inside, but I had to work. I was an assistant manager there and had hired some of the people that I knew. This wasn't my first job. I had worked at The Gap and a gas station close to Duke University, long before I found myself in an abusive relationship. While working at the gas station, this guy that played basketball at Duke would come in and ask me out week after week. I turned him down because he had big ears. That guy with the big ears went on to play for the NBA and became one of the top players. He ended up marrying a famous R&B singer, and they seem to have a loving, committed marriage.

While I worked in my new job, one of my friends that we called Big Tiff from school would help watch my daughter for me. Big Tiff didn't play! She was also in nursing school with me and knew that I was being abused and would say, "Tonya, I will kick his ass!" One night she came by the store while we were closing with baby girl. I was in the back, counting the cash registers when she arrived. Not thinking that it was a problem, I let them in. During this time, the manager and I weren't on good terms because if I didn't have anyone to watch my daughter, I would call out of work. When the manager found out that I had let them in the store, the next time I had to work, she was ready and waiting to fire me. It caught me off guard. I had worked hard in that disgusting store. Out of anger, I took the store keys and threw them at her head. She screamed and shouted, get out of here. I believe the only reason she didn't call the police was because my daughter was with me. This was another day that I didn't have a baby sister; she asked me to come in and turn in my keys. At this point, she had more than one reason to fire me, and she didn't hesitate.

When I walked out, I could have called my drug, but I didn't, and I had no idea what I was going to do now. The drug dealer would have taken care of everything, but I had to do this on my own. The struggle began. What saved us was that I still was receiving money from the man that I thought was my father, an educational benefit as a result of him having been disabled in the military. The checks were not enough to pay the rent, car payments, buy food, clothes, and meet our basic needs. I didn't have any money left to pay the babysitter that had been keeping baby girl during the day, while I was in class. Also, if you are wondering about the guy who my mother chose, well, he never even asked where she was nor offered any help. Another friend of mine, the guy that I met the summer before we left for college, stepped up. He was a huge help to me, and he had never stopped loving me and would watch baby girl for me so that I could go to class. One month I couldn't pay my rent and mother happened to call. Before I knew it, the rent was paid. Then later, I recall asking God what I was supposed to do now and went to the mailbox. In the mailbox was a $600 check. That might not seem like much now, but in the '90s that went a long way. The check was from the man my mother told me was my father when I turned 18. That was the first that I had heard from him. He wrote me a letter and told me that he had recently retired from the postal service and wanted to send me some money to help me out. He also asked me never to call his house. If I didn't need the money, I would have torn the check up and threw it in the trash. It hurt to read that in a letter from a man that I never had a chance to get to know. I was also responsible for all the rent because my roommate and I had gone our separate ways. That didn't come without a fight, literally. Our relationship had dissolved, one day, I came home, and she was cursing me out on the answering machine. She decided to tell me that she had hooked this girl up with this guy that I had been seeing that was in law school. It was a joke to her, and she laughed about it. I guess she thought that she would have left before I got back home. Well, the joke was on her! I recall busting in the bathroom while she was in the shower and dragging her out. A violent fight broke out, and I put her out of the house. Besides, she wanted to leave, so get out! She went next door and called family, that I realized much later in the day when I arrived home.

Who would have thought that our friendship would have come to this? We had grown apart as friends and relationships. I received a phone call one day from one of her family members who began to tell me how she shouldn't have to live with someone like me who had a baby. During this time, I was focused on my schoolwork. I was taking more than full-time hours, working full-time, and I was a full-time mother. My roommate, on the other hand, had met an older guy and spent most of her time there. I still didn't think that my daughter being there would have changed things so drastically because she had gone through something personal, and I was there for her. That is what we did for each other; she was my sister.

Nevertheless, I gave in and decided to let her out of the lease. Besides, this was the life path that I had chosen why should she have to change her lifestyle. Farewell to my dear friend, I wanted to share so much more with her in terms of how I was feeling, why I had to bring my baby with me, but I never got the chance. She had moved out and wanted nothing to do with the new arrangement. Now it was my baby girl and me against the world, trying to make our way. I believed in my heart that God was going to take care of us.

I soon found another job that paid a good salary. My baby girl had started kindergarten. Her face was bright and cheery. She was still the independent type and preferred to dress herself. My choice of clothes for her was from the gap. I made sure that her hair was done and that she had beautiful things. I could not imagine seeing her the way that I saw her the day when I knew I could not leave her behind. The only worry that I had now was, picking her up after school because I had to work. I had met someone, and I am ashamed to say. He was tall, very handsome, muscular with a large afro, and cooked for us regularly. People didn't have afros in the '90s, but it seemed to work for him. He was more handsome than any other guy that I had dated. At first, he appeared to be drama-free, he wasn't in college and spent most of his time with my daughter and me. He didn't care that I had a child and was putting forth an effort to help.

While at work one day, a tall, fair-skinned girl that was a familiar face on campus showed up on my job. She was beautiful, and people on campus were fond of her. She approached me and started to ask questions about Mr. Afro and my relationship. He wasn't drama free! He had dated her, but she admitted that they weren't together at that moment but wanted me to back away. They had been together for some time, and she was clearly in love, and I could understand why. Selfishly, I decided to maintain the relationship because I enjoyed his company, and besides, he was helping me out. Why would I give that up? Daily, he would ensure that my baby girl got in the house safe and waited with her until I got off work. He would ensure that she ate and had what she needed. Being such an old soul, she didn't like watching cartoons but preferred watching the news. He tried to change her mind, and she didn't like him.

I recall, one day, my baby girl being hesitant of him letting her in the house after school, and it concerned me. He called my job and said that she had locked herself in the bathroom. I later found out from her that she had wet her pants waiting to get in the house because he was late. She was very protective and private. I would agree in this matter, protect yourself, baby girl! To my knowledge, he never harmed her. My mother, on the other hand, couldn't stand him.

She called the house, and he answered. Mr. Afro had never answered my phone before, I was getting things out of the car, and he had just brought a Christmas tree to the house so that we could decorate. I was on the way in the house carrying bags and could hear my mother screaming through the phone, "GET OUT OF THERE!" My mother did not want to see me hurt every again. I would agree, it was more than I could handle. After that call, he stopped coming around. I believe his feelings were hurt. I never learned much about him and quite frankly didn't care. He was a loner who was quiet and humble.

Another day while I was at work, surprisingly, my old Kappa friend showed up at my job. I had not seen nor heard from him since he graduated. Being that he was older than me, he had left me behind and was pursuing his future. After not hearing from him and moving on in relationships, he was not someone that I thought about. He expressed that he still cared about me, but I told him that I was going to marry the guy that I had met the summer before starting school. We were an item now. When I stopped dating Mr. Afro, he stepped in and had started helping me with baby girl. We attempted to be intimate, but we could never seem to connect in that manner. It was quite frustrating to me, but I didn't give up on him. I wanted to change my life and was tired of all the drama. He was a good guy that had been drama free and always treated me with respect. Over the years, he had given me roses and never missed my birthday. It never mattered who I was seeing; he still gave me a gift. I was approaching my last semester and didn't want to do anything that would stop me from graduating. I did not graduate in May because I had to change my major. My life was about school now and not partying. Although he was kind to me we were missing the spark. We were never able to have the relationship that he wanted, no matter how hard we tried. After graduation we decided to remain friends. I stayed in Durham, while he returned to his hometown.

I remained friends with the sister of the guy that abused me, and somehow, I managed to avoid him. She was going through her own set of issues and I believe it brought us closer. She was stronger than me and had gone through more than I could have ever handled.

Times were changing, and so was the heart of my former roommate. She asked if we could meet one day, and we did, both apologizing. I loved her like a sister, and this is precisely what I needed in my life at this point. When I told her the things that I endured, and she shared some of her life changes, forgiveness was easy for both of us. I finally had my friend and sister back. I still had not broken ties with my ex's sister, and we were still hanging tight. I even went to the same hairstylist, but it led to me running into the drug dealer again while preparing for a hair show.

My life wasn't utterly boring; I still managed to have fun with my friends. We traveled out of the country now a couple of times to Cancun, where we had a fantastic time. Around this time, I was more selective with the men that I dated. I had met an NFL football player, and our time together was unmeasurable. We talked on the phone day and night. He had already gone to the super bowl and was in a Nintendo game. The only challenge was that he didn't live in Durham; he was in San Diego, California. The next time that I was planning to see him, I put in a lot of effort. I spent the entire day out trying to find the right look. I remember baby girl complaining that she was car sick, but I didn't think that meant that she was feeling sick until she had thrown up everywhere. That was precisely what I didn't need now. I didn't have much time and felt the burden of the responsibility. She couldn't help it, and at least she warned me, I just wasn't listening.

Later that night, I got dressed and went to the party. I managed to see my new NFL player. Word was traveling fast and had even made it back to my abusive ex, who was also at the party. Full of sarcasm, he asked if my new boyfriend could sign a football for him. I was so uncomfortable and didn't know what to expect. He was capable of doing anything. When NFL arrived, I stayed close and kept asking that we leave. I got him to leave early, but he thought it was because I wanted to get him to myself. That was the last thing that I wanted. I tried to approach him differently. We never parted and spent the next day together where he let me drive his convertible Mercedes around the town. For someone my age, I was blown away, thinking only about who he was and not who he was to me.

The hair show was coming up, and we had all planned to meet over my ex's sister's house before going to practice. We were still friends, and the entire gang was there while others were waiting at the practice location, even my old roommate. When I arrived at her apartment, my hairstylist informed me that she was driving my ex's car. We hadn't dated and the last time that I saw him was at the party, but the mention of his name made me uncomfortable in every way. I also had my daughter with me that evening. When we left out of the house and got in my car, the drug dealer appeared out of nowhere. He was with the girl that he had been living with, picking up his car. When he saw that I was there, he came over to my car in rage and began banging and kicking the side of the car where my daughter was sitting. My daughter started screaming and crying. I was frozen with fear and had no idea why I didn't just drive off. He didn't stop until his girlfriend started screaming stop, she has her daughter in the car. Everyone there saw him and just looked and went on about their business. When I finally got the nerve to drive off, I was so hysterical that I had to pull over on the side of the road while everyone that was headed to practice drove by. I managed to make it to the practice after I was sitting on the side of the road for a while. I couldn't stop shaking, and my baby girl was still crying. I was telling her that it was going to be okay and that she would never see him again.

After that night, I decided that my time in Durham had ended. I didn't feel like I had the friendships that I once believed that I had. My determination to leave turned into strength. Yes, God had kept us, but it was time to exercise some common sense. It was time to move on. That would be the only way that I would be able to get rid of this guy. Having a background and experience in retail, I applied over the phone to an electronic job opening in Arlington Virginia, located outside of DC for a manager position at Macy's Department Store. I did not expect that they would call me back, but they did. By this time, my mom had relocated back to Washington, DC, after all those years. There was no reason for her to stay in the house now that everyone was gone. My mother had managed to get herself back on her feet after losing my stepfather and finding out that he had cheated on her for nearly 13 years.

I drove up for an interview and was offered the job on the spot. That was all that I needed. My brother and his wife even offered to allow me to stay with them until I was able to find another place to live. His wife had helped me get another car when my Porsche became too costly to keep up. I needed a more economical car. She co-signed for the car, and every month, I would mail her the payment. I appreciated her support because she didn't have to help me.

Chapter 14

The Move

After getting the job offer, I found a couple who sublet my apartment. My NFL player came down that weekend as I prepared to move. He helped me financially get what I needed to move into storage. Then I placed everything that I could that was left in my car, my red Mitsubishi Mirage. It was far from the white Porsche that I had driven for years, but it was reliable. I was unable to fit a few items in my car, one of which my baby girl loved. Her supposed father had purchased her a life-sized teddy bear. The teddy bear had a large red bow by the ear and wore a sweatshirt covered in hearts. We had gone to the mall one day for her third birthday and walk by this bear. Baby girl just stopped and played with the bear, when we tried to leave, she had her first tantrum. She fell out on the floor and started kicking and crying! Before I knew it, we were leaving with this bear.

Thinking back in time, the guy that my mother had chosen had decided against college and preferred the street life instead. This was interesting since he did everything that he could to keep me away from my first. He called me one day and asked if I wanted to take a trip with him. This was after he had purchased the bear over the summer during my freshman year in college. I thought well maybe we can make this work when he felt that I had something that he needed, which was a car. We ended up taking a trip to New York. I had gone once when I was younger with my father and remembered how to get back. I would never be able to pull that off now!

After arriving in New York, he left me in the car for two hours, and when he returned, he said, "Let's go." I thought that we would spend some time in New York, but he meant let's get back to North Carolina, which was a nine-hour drive. He had driven there and wanted me to drive back. When I would speed up, he kept saying go the speed limit so that we don't get a ticket. When we finally made it home, I realized that he had used me to drug traffic with him. If we had gotten caught, I would have spent the rest of my life in jail and who would have been there for my baby girl. He only cared about himself. Mr. Good Guy was now Mr. Want to be Drug Dealer.

Nonetheless, during this move, we had to leave Teddy behind, and we got on the road. The car barely had room for my baby girl to sit, and after almost a 6-hour drive that should have taken four hours, we made it to Clinton, Maryland. I should have felt at home since we were back together again with my two nephews, but unfortunately, it didn't. My mother lived in DC, which was about 30 minutes away. I was thankful to my brother and his wife for taken us in, although I never felt comfortable being there. I'm sure that they thought otherwise, besides they were doing a great deed, right? They had given up space in their new home for my brother's side of the family, and I felt it every day that I was there.

I never seemed to be able to have the relationship with my brother's wife that should have existed since she was there for me when I first found out that I was pregnant. There was always some friction there between us. Have you ever met someone that when they do a good deed, it's like, look at what I did or someone that wants to remind you that I helped you when you were down and out! That was her actions toward me…

While living in their home, I worked my new job at the Macy's Department store as a floor manager for nearly a month. Before moving, I had worked retail for two years and had never experienced the difficulty that I had with this job. I was working hard and had to be there at 4 am every other week to participate with the jump team. We had to stock and remerchandise the store before it opened at 10 am. That may seem like a lot of time, but we are talking about a large Department Store with three floors. In the mornings before going into the store, I would sit downstairs in the mall while I waited for the doors to open with tears in my eyes. I had so much regret. I thought that if I had been more focused in school, I would have my dream job, which was to work for the FBI. I felt so low and was disappointed in myself. My mother never said anything, but deep down, I knew that she was hoping for more. I met quite a few people while working there but seemed to return to Durham every time I heard that a party was happening. Now how can you leave a place if you keep going back?

After a month, I was recruited by two managers to go and work for a new store in the mall. It was smaller but very stylish, a boutique. Walking in there had its challenges. I know that I am a beautiful woman, fearfully and wonderfully made, but during that time, I was the girl with the country accent, trying to look fashionable in my country girl attire. It was nothing high fashion about me. I was an assistant manager there at a store that had only 3 locations at the time, New York, and Rodeo Drive.

Celebrities shopped the store for their appearances, and we would provide clothes for the women entertainers on the set of the Black Entertainment Television, BET. Yes, this is how high fashion this store was! Consequently, they would give us tickets to the events that they had. I recall the night when I felt second class. The event was over the top, and every celebrity that you can think of was going to be there. Unfortunately, someone had to stay back and work. Being selected to work wasn't my issue, hearing the comment; let the country girl work is what wounded by heart. While, working there I became close with a friend that would one day follow her dream and become an attorney.

It seems that I was working most of the time and didn't think that leaving my daughter at my brothers was an issue since they were home and baby girl would just play with my niece. Until one day, my brother's wife told me that I needed to find a babysitter. I didn't understand this because they were home when she got out of school, along with everyone else. She was right; it was my responsibility, so I found a lady in the neighborhood. While we were staying with my brother, baby girl and my niece had their own set of challenges. They would fuss and fight over toys. When we left Durham, we didn't have room in the car for any of my baby girl's toys. I found that this started happening more and more frequently. Yes, I know that kids will fight. The problem that I had was that when someone was to blame, it was always my baby girl.

There was a feeling of separation in the house; it felt like it was them and us. My nephews had a room in the basement of this house that was unfinished. It was dark, cold with no paint nor carpet. They left a home situation to be treated like they were a bother. They also were punished and discipline frequently by my brother. It was apparent that he didn't know any other way. I know he didn't have it easy, growing up during a time when my mother thought that discipline was the only way. My brother had once abused drugs but turned his life around, giving his life to Christ and was on his second marriage to a woman that my mother didn't meet until the day they got married.

I had no idea who this woman was. The summer before they got married on a visit to the city, I had an opportunity to hang out with him, and I met a different woman. She stayed the night and gave me a blue poodle that he had won for her at the fair. So, when I met this woman, his current wife, I was confused. She was not as lovely or kind as the other woman. This woman was arrogant. After they were married, my brother brought her to NC to my mother's house, and the entire time she was there, she turned her nose up. They visited during the summer when my bothers oldest son was there as well. I had a nephew that was older than me. In the summer, my mother would send for him to come down to get him the things that he needed for school. She would do that for both of his children because my brother did nothing to take care of them. When my brother was home, he took his new wife to the mall, and she began to pick out the different things that she wanted. My older nephew and I tagged behind. I would hear my nephew say, "How can he buy her anything when he has yet even to acknowledge why I am here and what I need." He was right, and I could see the sadness in his son's eyes as he searched for love from his father. If only my brother could see him, I mean really see his heart. This young man had been through and seen a lot in his lifetime. Understanding the streets was an understatement; for him, it was about surviving, and he learned quickly to hold his own.

I loved the summers when my older nephew or dimples as I like to call him would spend with us. He became a staple in the neighborhood and was more like a Big Brother to me. I love him so much! Even today, he still looks out for me and has the biggest, kindest heart of anyone that you would ever want to meet. You would think that his heart would be tainted and hardened by everything that he has endured. He lost daughters who were trapped in a car while playing outside on a hot summer day and guess who was not there for him, you guessed right, his father. He was not there the way that he needed his father to be. I don't know how he does it, how he continues to smile. It was a rough time for him, and we all recognize that they were a gift from God who was returned to the heavenly father. Dimples, you are my heart, and my brother and there is no way that I can ever tell your story, so I digress as it would take most of my book to talk about a life of someone like you that has overcome and made it through the fire.

My brother and his new wife's trip to the country left a bad taste in everyone's mouth, and there was a rocky road ahead. I personally, while staying with them, always felt like I needed to keep one eye open. There were times when I felt comfortable enough to express how I was feeling with her. I would express my discontentment with being a mother; at times, I thought it was taking me away from life. At that point in my life, I just wanted to have a good time. I would confide in her not knowing that one day she would remind me of what I said and what she did for me. I sincerely appreciate them both, but I can't pretend that I ever felt the warmth of family while staying there.

One day at work, a beautiful young girl walks in and comes directly over to me. She had perfect skin, long hair and sizable breast that would turn heads. She asked me about Mr. Producer. Someone had shared that I was dating him. Little did I know we had a lot in common because she was seeing someone that was in the same group. We would spend years traveling, partying, going to the Soul-Train awards, walking red carpets and on tour with our boyfriends. We had whirlwind experiences, road trip after road trip; we watched groupies rush to the hotel after the concerts, always wondering how they knew where they were staying.

We became the best of friends with her standing by me through difficult times. Through my on and off again relationship with Mr. Producer, she was always right there. She was older than me and would always say "T, you have got to move on". She even did the unthinkable once when I lost a job. She had gone on an interview for the job and turned the offer down. I do not know anyone that would have done what she did next. She indicated that the job was not for her but that she knew someone that was perfect for the job and they hired me. During this time, Mr. Producer did not even offer me a slice of bread, nothing…

One birthday while I was on yet another hiatus with Mr. Producer, I had met a guy that was 10 years younger than me one Howard homecoming weekend. That relationship leads me and my home-girl to New York. Talk about a night to remember. She knew everyone when I had no idea who's house, we were over. In this case I will just say W was the group. Out of all the rappers that I've been around I will say that they were the most respectful. I ended up in the studio the next day with a second opportunity to record on an album that would later go platinum. I blew it! My self-esteem wasn't where it needed to be, and I didn't give it my best. I can still hear my home-girl's voice as we returned home... "T, as she called me, what happened?!"

Chapter 15

Returning to the Well

O ne day I received a call from my ex, the drug dealer, after managing to escape. What fool would have taken his call, well me, that's who! I've learned that abused women blame themselves and often think about what they could have done differently to make the abuser love you more. Well, he had relocated from Durham to Atlanta, and now had new girlfriends. Yes, that is plural; some things never change. He was making even more money than ever before, after leaving Durham, running from the police. His crew was dismantled, two had already been arrested. He had started a record label and had his very first hip hop artist, who was one of his dear friends. Remembering that I could sing, he reached out for me to record on the album.

My brother's wife refused to watch baby girl for me, so I had to find another option. If you recall, when I was in high school, singing was a passion of mine. I was pretty good actually and would win the local talent shows. It was a known fact that I could sing. This was an opportunity that I didn't want to miss. I asked the neighborhood babysitter if she could keep baby girl for me. She agreed but wanted a substantial payment that I didn't have. To pay her, I wrote a fraudulent gift card to her from the store where I worked. I am ashamed, but this is an example of how God has changed my life.

I had stardom in my eyes for this trip to Atlanta. Although I didn't want to see him, I wanted the opportunity to sing in the studio. When I arrived, much hadn't changed with him. I found myself in his room on the floor, use your imagination. He was determined to have sex with me. I recall afterward going into the bathroom and crying. When he finished, he said, "Hurry up and get yourself together, my girlfriend is on her way here!"

Well, this brought back memories; it wasn't the first time I had been in Atlanta with the drug dealer. The first time we were here was before we started to have all the drama in the relationship. The first trip consisted of us partying and buying out the VIP section. It was nothing to spend thousands in one night on champagne and alcohol. Before the club his sister and I shopped and purchased everything that we wanted from the Versace store and others without limits. It all seems exciting, but it still came with a price of abuse. The night after the club, his sister and I hung out with a couple of NFL players and didn't return until the next day. When I arrived, the drug dealer was waiting and dragged me down the hall of the hotel. If you are reading this, it is not worth it. I recall, in recent years, a young lady was bragging about someone that she knew that had more than five Chanel bags and every other designer bag that you could imagine. Then two weeks later, she explained how the young lady had been murdered in the car with her boyfriend. I thank God every day that I am Still Standing!

When I arrived at the studio, he left me there to record with the Producer. My life changed forever! This was my first-time recording, and the Producer felt that I needed some encouragement. Mind you; this is someone that I never met before. While in the booth, he turned off all the lights and came into the booth. He said he was going to help me, and before I knew it, he was performing oral on me. Okay, this was a first! I had never experienced this before, and no, I didn't stop him. I was so afraid of getting caught that I just continued to sing.

That night, we all went out to the club, and I watch while my ex paraded his new girlfriend in front of me. She was different from the one that I saw him with earlier that day. After the club, we headed out to the Waffle House to eat. While we were there, my ex noticed how the Producer had been flirting with me. When we got back to the house, while sitting in the living room, he decided to address it. Then the animal that I once knew appeared, once again. He took a Big Gulp cup of soda and launched it in my direction. He had zero respect for me. This man could care less who was around nor how he made me feel. The feelings of rejection and low self-esteem were there all over again. The Producer had given me his number. At this point, I just needed to get away from this crazy man. I left and went outside to call the Producer from the payphone. After talking for a while, I went back inside the house, and by this time, my ex had left the house, and the next day I returned home.

When I returned to Clinton, Maryland, it was back to what had become the closest to normal that I would have for some time. The house shut down early most nights by 9 pm, and there were to be no phone calls as everyone was asleep by this time. I spent the next few months when I got home mostly close to midnight, under the covers whispering with my new friend, the Producer. He was very comical, and I was always laughing. At that time, I had no idea who he was but later learned that he was famous. He had starred in a movie and produced several hit records that had received Grammys. I continued to work, pay rent where I was, and save money. The situation with my niece and my daughter continued. Not to mention on Sundays, I was required to attend church. This was something that I hadn't done since I left for college, although it was a regular part of my life early on. When I was younger, I was excited about going to church. My daughter was the same way when she first came to stay with me while I was finishing college. On Sunday mornings, she would get up and put her dress on, then come to my room and beg to go to church. I would just yell at her to go back to bed. Church wasn't something that I was interested in anymore.

After my mother gave her life to Christ, our lives went from her playing cards all night into the morning to chasing evangelist from one tent revival to the next. We were in a church anywhere from three to four days a week. There was no way out of attending. She also started her own church, and my stepfather would drive the van while we picked up the people to attend. I despised that church van. There was this Ugly boy that would try to fondle me every single time. I would have to fight him off there and back. This was before I had even lost my virginity, and I was too afraid to tell my mother. What I didn't know then and know now, is that I was physically abused. This Ugly guy as I will continue to refer to him because he was, and it would not have made a difference if he wasn't. The point was I was a young little girl who was being touched. My mother never thought about that; she was only worried about my great uncle, who was a known child predator getting close to me when it was happening right under her nose. Why was I a silent victim? I have lived with many hidden emotions for most of my life, and I am glad to be able to release these demons on paper now because I am still standing.

It was time for me to make another move. After staying at my brother's for about six months, I had found my own place. It was a lovely two-bed and, two-bathroom apartment in a beautiful suburb in Upper Marlboro, Maryland. I transferred baby girl's school and the same day that I received my keys was the same day that we moved out, again with everything that we could pack in my red Mitsubishi Mirage. That night we slept on the floor on a blanket or pallet as they called it in the country. When I left Durham, I left my furniture behind.

Thankfully my brother helped me get my furniture, and soon we had our belongings. I finally felt like I had a sense of belonging, a place to stay that I could call our own. I had beautiful furniture that my mother had given me. When she was depressed, shopping and re-furnishing, the house was her relief. In the battle of one of her down, upturns, she gave me the current living room furniture and the bedroom set from my room.

This apartment was an upgrade from my college community. There I had to take my clothes behind the building to the laundromat. Here I had a washer and dryer. We also had a pool, tennis courts and a racquetball court. Most people wouldn't care about a racquetball court, but in college, when everyone decided to take bowling for the required credit, I took racquetball. I enjoyed racquetball and would go to the court and play. I was still going back and forth to Durham during this time for every party. I wanted to hold on to my friends. They would come to my house often as well. My mother hated it when they came to stay with me and would say that they were just using me.

Finally, my Producer friend wanted me to make a trip to New York. He called and had purchased me an airline ticket, and this is when it began. When in New York, we would stay in hotels, and the frequency of my visits back and forth became more and more. When he was on tour, I would meet him there as well. He became like another type of drug to me. I couldn't get enough, and when I would get mad with him, he would not call me for weeks at a time. I soon learned to keep my mouth closed, which I now realize was mental abuse. None of my friends liked him because of how crazy I was about him. There was nothing anyone could say to me to stop me from talking or being with him. From hotel to hotel, from tour stop to tour stop, I had to be there!

I remember one night; he had given me his room key before they hit the stage and told me not to let him beat me back to the hotel. Well, I had brought a friend along and ended up getting to the room after he had gotten there. Oh boy, I had no idea what he was going to do. He had never shown any violence towards me, but I wasn't sure what to expect. I had tears in my eyes as I stood outside of his room, knocking on the door. He made me beg and apologize for not being there in his comical way. After that, he let me in the room. This relationship roller coaster went on for over ten years.

When we would be on a hiatus, I started to see other people. I met this one guy that wasn't my type, but I enjoyed the time that we would spend together. One night he took me to an NBA game, and after the game, we ended up having dinner with the entire team. The night was comical. It seemed that I was the only one eating; as a joke, some of the players started to order food and send it to me as if I had requested it all. We had fun times until later when I had to share something disturbing with him. Today, I watch him from afar with major regret as he spoils his wife; together with him, she has become a successful entrepreneur, and they have a huge mansion in the suburbs of Maryland. I also met an older, corny white man on my job that loved my every move. When he walked, he wobbled like a duck from side to side. I shouldn't say this because he was very kind man. My heart had become hardened. He would stop by every day and bring me coffee, breakfast, or anything that I wanted. I wasn't interested in him at all, but the benefits were hard to refuse.

We were never intimate, not even with a kiss, but I would allow him to take me on trips. One year he took my daughter and me when she was nine years old to London, England, over the Thanksgiving holiday. This man was madly in love with me, and I was taking advantage of him. Six months before that, he had taken me on a cruise to the Caribbean, and one of the stops was in Nassau Bahamas. While we were there, I had him buying me Gucci and Fendi. I had decided that if he was going to be with me, it had to be worth my while. The trip to London was really for my daughter. Baby girl seemed like a native of the country by the time we arrived, she had picked up the accent and was on constant repeat saying, "Tea, Coffee."

While in London, we toured all the major tourist attractions, the opera and the very first showing of the Lion King, but nothing seemed to excite my Baby Girl like seeing the palace jewels. She admired the crowns worn by the queen and the ones before her. It was something special about being there with her, besides her middle name was Victoria, and maybe it meant something only time will tell. The only disappointment for her on this trip was on Thanksgiving Day. Baby Girl had grown up with the elaborate spreads of food and was not one to miss a meal. The joke was that people didn't mind taking her out to eat because they knew that she would clean her plate, and it never failed. This year instead of her favorites, glazed ham, macaroni and cheese, and candied yams, she had a grill cheese sandwich, plated with the edges cut off. The look on her face was priceless, as she began to ask where the rest of it was. I didn't see a smile on her face again until she was eating a cheeseburger from McDonald's. Every time I look at that picture with her cheeks full and her smiling from ear to ear, I recall her love for good food. I emphasize good food because if it weren't, she would tell you or frown. Baby girl still had the idea in her mind that she had to clean her plate even if she didn't like the food. My mother did not allow food to be thrown away. Returning from London, I thought things would go back to the norm, but when I checked my voicemail, things would never be normal for me again.

So much time has passed; I even transferred to a different apartment in another building after my apartment was broken into. The summer when my daughter was away, I decided to upgrade my living room furniture and had placed it outside on the patio. One night after getting home from a date, I went directly to bed, but at about 6:00 that morning, someone was banging on my door. When I opened the door, a lady with her dog was asking me my name and said, "I need to show you something. Your purse is behind the building." I was so tired that it was hard for me to translate what she was saying. Did I drop my purse before coming inside the house? I thought I had placed my purse on the kitchen countertop. Well, I went to the sliding glass door and wouldn't you know it. Someone had broken into my place. The glass was shattered in Baby Girls' room, and in the back of the building was my purse. They had cut the inside lining and taken my wallet and shades but left the purse lying on the ground. This was an amateur! I had just gotten this Gucci bag only days before, and it was more valuable than anything that he had taken out of my purse. Forget the purse; now, I was terrified.

When I went back inside the house, I realized that whoever it was in the house when I arrived home. Earlier that day, I had the carpets cleaned, and you could see where his footprints had walked all around my bed. It was something about that night. I had an eerie feeling when getting ready for bed and went to make sure that the bar was down on the sliding door. I then place the covers over my head and repeated Psalm 23 repeatedly until I fell asleep. God was protecting me that night. He was in the house when I arrived home and had taken my purse off the kitchen counter. The toys in my daughters' room had been knocked over when he came through the window. The police said that there would have been no way that I wouldn't have heard him. After that, I had alarms placed throughout the apartment and transferred to the other side of the complex. Thank God I was safe! I can't imagine what my life would be like now if I would have had to add something so damaging to everything that had already damaged me.

After returning from London, I had several missed calls from my OBGYN and voicemail messages asking me to call them immediately. Before the trip, I had gone for my regular yearly exam. When I called the office, they would not tell me what was wrong; they would only tell me that I need to make an appointment to come in. I had no idea but was thinking maybe the pre-cancerous cells that were burned off my uterus in college had returned. When I got to the office, I was shocked at what they had to say.

Mr. Producer and I met after one of our long hiatuses when he was in town for a show. He was just returning from Japan. Things between us had changed. After moving out of my brothers, Mr. Producer didn't call me for almost three months, and I had no idea why. He typically would only do that if I had made him angry; it was his way of punishing me. I found out from a college friend, who was from New York, why I hadn't heard from him. Because he was well known, he couldn't hide the fact that he had just had a newborn baby girl. Yes, this guy had an entire family in New York. A woman that he had dated for most of their young adult lives. She had a son by him early in his career when he was still struggling in the projects until they made it out. He had been with this woman through thick and thin, he wasn't leaving her, and she wasn't leaving him. So, I asked myself, who was I to him? The answer was nobody, but another piece of meat was all I could think of at the time.

The news about the newborn should have changed my thinking and the way I felt about him, but I was too far gone. I continued to talk to him, and we continued to have sex every time that we saw each other to include after he had gotten back from Japan. The doctors' report yielded two sexually transmitted diseases, and they asked me the question. Have you been tested for HIV? My heart dropped. People weren't as knowledgeable about this disease as they are now, and there was a huge fear factor. When you're asked that question, you know just how severe the matter is. My half-sister supported me through this crisis because I couldn't tell anyone. It was and still is the most fearful situation that I have ever had to deal with personally. My half-sister helped me find the Whitman Walker Clinic.

I never knew that I had a half-sister until my mother called me at work one day when I was still living in Durham, working as a store manager at Contempo Casuals. The man that she said was my father when I was 18 and that had sent me the $600 and asked that I never call his house, had passed away. After he passed, while the family was putting away his belongings, my half-sister found letters that he and my mother had written each other over my entire lifetime. When my mother told me about him, she never shared this part of the story. When I arrived in Maryland, I met her for the first time. I wasn't interested in meeting nor talking to her. My mother, when she called my job, begged me to speak to her.

When I did, I wasn't very friendly as I wasn't interested in knowing this man nor anyone associated with him after he said never to contact him. When I met her, she was awkwardly tall for a woman with huge feet and a gigantic butt. It was apparent to me that I got the pretty genes from my mother. I recalled her having colored contact lenses and not being very fashionable. She ended up being very kind to Baby Girl and me, but there was always this struggle between us. My half-sister, who I had practically just met, expected to be my best girlfriend and hang out with my friends and me. When I didn't invite her, one day she asked was it because she didn't have designer clothes.

What she didn't understand was that this wasn't easy for me. I had spent my summers in Greensboro with who I loved, and thought were my grandparents. When I stopped going to Greensboro at 13, I assumed it because I overheard my grandmother say how dark-skinned I was. My grandfather just replied and said she looks like me. My grandmother had even taken me to the hair salon with her and requested that they put a jheri curl in my hair because she said that my hair was nappy. When I stopped getting invited, growing up, I thought I wasn't good enough to be there with them anymore. Besides, one of my Aunts had a daughter, and she had hair down the middle of her back. My favorite Aunt, who I would call mom, loved me no matter what. She took me everywhere that she went. She belonged to the first Greek organization that was founded at Howard University, and her standards for my conduct as it related to me were reasonably high. I remember being around her and her sorority sisters, and she would tell me to sit up straight and to put my shoulders back. This sister, who I had just met, was now judging me based on my outward appearance and did not see my heart. Our relationship was a continuous tug of war; she likes me, and then again maybe not.

As I entered the Whitman Walker Clinic, it was old with grey tones, and the atmosphere was somber. Everyone seemed to have the same weight of life on their shoulders as I did. I expected to go in an get the test, and leave. Well, it didn't work that way. They started a session about sexually transmitted diseases and safe sex. The details were far beyond things that I ever thought about doing or had experienced in my life, so in my mind, I placed myself in a different category. Basically, to say that I'm not one of them. They were focusing on same-sex couples. Initially, this wasn't a concern, Mr. Producer and I had experienced anal a couple of times, but it wasn't something that I liked to do. What concerned me was his reaction to me telling him no. After I said no, he decided that he didn't want to be intimate with me. Also, I questioned in my mind from time to time his responses to me sexually. Things between us had changed. Years had passed by, and while he was on yet another one of his hiatuses, I found out that he had gotten married. He kept this secret from me and never told me. He hurt me so badly, but I allowed the relationship to continue for over ten years. I wouldn't let him go.

When the presentation was complete, I had my test and then had to wait two weeks for the results. The day that I returned, I was so afraid. I had cried nearly every day. When I told Mr. Producer about the first results that I received from my OBGYN, his response was he caught these sexually transmitted diseases from the Chinese food that he had eaten. I was beyond angry, and he stood his ground even to say that it was on the news in New York. Clearly, he thought that I was Boo Boo the Fool! I should hate him, but for some reason, I was never able too. He never wished me Happy Birthday, nor celebrated anything special with me. I always felt that it was about him. He always said, "I know when your birthday is." It was a sad day for him because he had lost his brother on the same day. The only thing that made me feel special was when we were together. The need for touch had stemmed from when I was a young girl, in a home where hugs and the words I love you were never said.

Today I get my results. Walking back in this grey, dark and gloomy place felt like the walk of death. I had dated others when we were on our many breaks, but I was always safe with them. Except in one instance, a guy that I was spending quite a bit of time with, the condom slipped off, and we didn't realize it until later. I would have to share these results with him. How embarrassing! He was a wholesome guy, an engineering graduate from the University of Maryland College Park. The Wholesome guy would cook me dinner and had taken me out on a few dates. Was I so low that now I was destroying the lives of others, the way my life was being destroyed?

At the Whitman Walker Clinic, I was placed in a room and asked to wait. I waited and waited; it felt like I was slowly dying in the inside. When the attendant entered the room with his enveloped, he asked the question, "How are you doing" and I just started crying. Then he gave me my results, "Your test came back negative!" I fell to my knees and was crying like a five-year-old child. After I got myself together, he said, "You were really worried, huh?" I began to explain to him how I had dated this Producer in the entertainment industry. I knew that there were other women, besides when they were on tour, the girls would find out what hotel they were staying in and would knock on every door in groups, might I add until finding the room of one of the artists that they wanted to party with. One night when I was there, I recall his boys coming to the room to get him while he explained that I was there. Now, what do you think was happening when I wasn't there? A man traveling the world, with money and popularity, was hard to resist for a girl that had stars in her eyes. I had been that girl once, but after going through this, I was determined to change my life. The attendant offered me condoms, and I remember the day that the man who I thought was my father did the same. This time I accepted them gratefully. Living on this dangerous edge was over.

When your life starts to flash in front of you, we are reminded where our help comes from. Living the life that I have now lived for all my 20's, quickly approaching my 30's had consisted of me making the same mistakes repeatedly. I am reminded today of the parable the woman at the well in John 4:4-42. I have always been intrigued by her story. People tend to focus on her discretions and the fact that she just kept going back to the well. I felt like I was the woman at the well. No matter what these men would do to me, I continued to return to the well. What was I searching for, and would I ever find it?

I immediately changed some things in my life. For one, I had stopped talking to Mr. Producer; I cut my hair and changed my wardrobe. I wanted to look different from how I had ever presented myself. I tried to hide from the Wholesome guy but had to tell him to get tested for sexually transmitted diseases. He ended up testing negative, but we never dated again. During this time, Baby Girl was so worried about me. I was taking a lot of naps and was depressed. I also went to share this with my mom, not even knowing how she would respond, but I needed moral support. Surprisingly, she did not judge me and shared with me how, when she was pregnant with me, the man that I thought was my father had placed her in the same situation. My mother explained how worried she was that I would be born blind or with some abnormality. She also told me not to be hard on myself but to stop giving my body away to these men. I cried, and she hugged me as she had never hugged me before.

Later closer to the end of the year, I heard a knock on my door. I wasn't expecting company and didn't have family or friends that would just show up unannounced. Baby girl being the mature young lady or little momma as we called her, made sure that I got the door. We had alarms, so we weren't too worried. When I opened the door, for the first time, stood Mr. Producer in a silver fur coat with a smile. I wasn't smiling, although there was something in me that said he cared. When he looked at me, he seemed shocked. I had cut off all my hair and was wearing it very short.

The person that he had known for most of her 20's was slowly disappearing. I wanted and needed to change my life. It amazes me how God works. For a few years, I stopped all the partying and searching for someone to watch Baby Girl. It was okay, and I could never say that I hadn't had an incredible run. Every year in May for a total of six years, my girls and I from Durham had traveled to Cancun, Mexico. The years that we spent traveling there are separate books within themselves. I partied with famous rappers on yachts and road on the back of scooters with them through the streets of Mexico. I even partied with famous actresses; people known in the industry world. We had this saying on these trips, "What happens in Cancun, stays in Cancun," and we took this to heart.

On one of my trips, while walking around Daddy-O's, this guy walked up to me and put a $100 bill down my shirt. When I tried to give it back and rolled my eyes, he just encouraged me to go and buy myself a drink. We exchanged numbers on this trip and stayed in touch. When returning to the states, we talked, and finally connected. He lived in Philadelphia and would get me a train ticket to come up and see him. He managed a couple of artists in the industry and was well known and connected. On my first trip there, we went to this house that I now know was a trap house to hear this guy rap. The guy was terrific, I had learned to decipher between good and bad music, having dated Mr. Producer for so long.

Apparently, this guy was so good, the next week, he was in NY recording with Roc-A-Fella records. It's too bad, though, because although he was a mastermind rapper, he could not control his temper, and as a result, the career was rocky. He did manage to put out a few records and a couple of videos. People loved this guy! I even recall them being on tour, and I went to meet them in Baltimore. I ended up taking them to the airport in the new Lexus Coupe that my Philadelphia friend helped me buy. I will refer to him as The Manager in this chapter. He liked to spoil me, and when we were together, it wasn't just about having sex. We would have dinner and go shopping on my trips to Philly. During this time, the Christian Dior saddle bags had become my staple handbag of choice, and I had three different colors. I never dated multiple people at the same time but would find myself in another man's arms whenever I felt rejected by Mr. Producer.

Mr. Producer had also gotten married but would continue to deny it, year after year. He would even wear a wedding ring from time to time. Every time that I would see him, the chemistry and love between us would die even more. We had taken so many hiatuses that it became a norm to me now. The only thing that was different is that I still could not deny him sexually until now. When he was at my house, it was uncomfortable for me. One reason is that I didn't bring men into my home with Baby Girl. She was a gift to me. Through her, I was learning how to love myself. For the early part of her life, I disliked the fact that I was a young teenage mom. One day when getting out of the car for school, she looked at me like she did every day and said: "Mommy, I love you." I don't know what made this day any different from the rest, but I heard her in a way that I never heard her before, responding, "I love you too." Baby Girl was one that would greet everyone with a big hug and smile. Often when she would hug me, I didn't know how to respond. Looking back, it seemed that the only way that I felt like I could give intimacy was too, give myself away to another man. Did I have Daddy issues, Mother issues, or all the above? It was all the above for me, and it started when I was the little girl in my room, crying and asking God why my mother didn't love me. From this day forward, I would love Baby Girl with all of me. I put her first in every aspect of my life. It was time for us to get out of this perpetual cycle of life that I had placed us in, and besides, I want to live. It is only by the grace of God that I am still standing and healthy.

We did not have sex that night while Mr. Producer was at the house. When he left, it was like I closed the door to my heart that day. My feelings for him would never be the same. I am not saying that I would never see him again, but the feelings were never the same. He no longer had control over me. Change comes slowly sometimes; even the Woman at the well after returning to the same place and same thing again and again, finally found love.

Chapter 16

She's Gone

My mother and I didn't always have the best relationship. She seemed to realize my efforts to change my life around. I had even started back going to church. My brother was now a Pastor of a church in Pasadena, Maryland. The location was about a 1 ½ to 2-hour drive for me depending on the day of the week and traffic. I was so determined to change my life around and was participating in the church choir, and Baby Girl was part of the dance ministry and cheerleading squad. These were her pastimes that she began when she was in kindergarten while we lived in Durham. One of my employees from Contempo Casual that worked for me had taken a liking to Baby Girl and had placed her on the cheerleading squad that she coached at the boys and girls club. She had also started taking dance with my niece when we first relocated from North Carolina. It was evident to me that she had a bright future ahead of her, and I didn't want her to waste it the way that I had wasted mine.

I spent my weekends either at home or at church. I had also joined Ministers in Training (MIT). The closer I got to God, the more I knew he was calling me to lead others to Christ. I had changed everything about myself that I believed people needed to see, Yes, I said people. I wore these boxy, dressy church suits, that were nice but not my style. As my brother's wife would say, and you will see later in the chapters, "She was teaching me how to dress appropriately." While attending my brothers' church, I was being taught with a strong iron hand and kept in a box; I was learning nothing about the love of God and only about the wrath of God. I will later get to know that God doesn't judge us from the outside and that the holy spirit and the word of God is what guides change in our lives. My mother had visited my brother's church once and felt that God was leading her to give a lady in the church a prophetic word from God.

The lady, a member of my brother's church, shared the word with him, but he did not like the fact that his mother did not go through him first. After that my mother did not go back to the church. What I found to be interesting is that my brother initially said that God had called him to Baltimore, and as a result, he had been going into the inner city and having service. My mother was always welcome to attend the services when he was in the high school auditorium. Things changed; I guess when he was assigned to be the Pastor of a storefront church in Pasadena, Maryland. Based on the events that had taken place, I must ask, wasn't God the same in the high school as he was in the storefront. My mother having been bold before knowing Christ demonstrated the same boldness in the faith. She believed that if God told her to do something, she was going to do it, whereas my brother felt that there was a protocol.

My life now was focused around the church. In 2003, I told my mother that I was going to preach my first sermon, and I remember that she just looked at me. I was expecting her to be excited and supportive, but I received the opposite from her. Did she see and know something that I didn't? I had settled down so much during this time that I wasn't even celebrating my birthday this year. Did God say that we couldn't have a good time? My mother called me earlier that day after speaking to her. The next thing that I knew about three hours later, she was walking up three flights of stairs with a platter of food, a birthday cake, and a gift. I'm not sure how she knew that I wasn't going to celebrate my birthday this year. I will never forget this day. When I opened the door, my eyes were filled with tears. How did she know? My mother was there to celebrate my life. I think that she was trying to tell me something indirectly without going against what I was learning under my brother.

Also, during this time, my brother's wife was going to minister her first sermon and was having trouble preparing her sermon. So, she called me up, and I helped her determine or gave which is more like the truth her sermon title. My first sermon was "Sin the Enemy of God." When God gives you a message to teach others, I am a living witness that you are the first student. I soon learned after spending over half of my life stuck in the wilderness what this meant. My mother did not come to hear me speak that night, but I tried to spend more time with her, and she would ask Baby Girl and me to stay over from time to time. She was not attending a dedicated church, only visiting. For over ten years after my mother was saved and went into ministry, she traveled by request for revivals. My mother had ministered from Fayetteville NC to Washington, DC, with stops in between. She was well known in Wilson and surrounding cities for how God would use her to lay hands on the sick as well as her style of preaching. My mother was very much like my great aunt Leona Vick her first Pastor.

When called to minister, she did not take her assignments lightly. I recall my mother going on a dry fast, that is no food nor water for five days at a time. She would go into the guest bedroom with a bucket, her oil, and her bible. The bucket was used when she needed to use the bathroom. So, to see my mother denied or questioned by my brother when she believed God had led her to give someone a prophetic word caused division. The family was divided now. My mother and my brother's wife were even more estranged now in the sense that she did not visit them, and they did not visit her. My mother no longer went over for Holiday dinners, but I would go because, at the time, I felt that my mother had caused the division. When I look back now, I would have never hurt my mother in that manner and would soon learn exactly how she felt.

As my mother got older, her mental and physical health declined. I believe the rejection caused her to go back into depression. I was taking her to her doctors' visits, paying her bills, and buying the groceries for her house. One day I asked my brother for help, and he lied to me and said that he had another commitment. When I was speaking to his wife, she confirmed and agreed with me that he just didn't want to be bothered. For me to get my brother to start helping me with our mother, I had to threaten him with telling his church members, if he did not. Even after, my brother would only go over if my mother needed him to do something. My second oldest brother, who had spent over half of his life in jail, had a child-like mindset, did nothing to help, and was in a world of his own. My oldest sister went missing for two years after relocating to Baltimore. My mother had walked the street and inside drug-houses looking for her. The last time we saw her, she had stopped by my mother's when she still lived in DC off Martin Luther King Avenue. My mother had asked that I bring her some clothes, a coat and if I could do her hair.

My sister had been a beautiful woman with an amazing curvy body that we would call a Beyoncé body today. She had destroyed her body with drugs, a heroin addiction that she would not be able to escape. Her body was covered with sores, but when I saw her, she was trying to get better. She had recently been hospitalized due to an open wound. On this day, after I did her hair, she asked if I could give her a ride to The House of Ruth, where she was staying, a shelter for women. I wasn't willing to help her; I was self-centered and selfish. I grew up being afraid of my sister after seeing her show up wearing layers of trash bags, smelling like rotten meat and screaming during the night as my mother sat with her to kick her drug habit. What I know now that I didn't realize then is that she was tormented by life demons that kept her going back to the one thing that allowed her to escape. My sister had been molested at a very young age by multiple men. She engaged in a relationship at 15 years old that led her to this addiction. The fact that both of her brothers were abusing heroin didn't help any.

My mother's depression included rejection and grief. She had lost two daughters now, one who was murdered and my sister that was missing had been dead for two years. One day while I was at work, I was on the internet playing around with this new site called Ancestry. com. I entered my youngest sister's name, and it gave me the date and location of her death. I also found my grandmother, so I started to search on different versions of my oldest sister's name. I entered her birth name and her maiden name because she had once been married. I found nothing until I typed a combination of them both in the search bar and could not believe my eyes. It said deceased and provided a social security number. I called my mother and asked if she could give me her social, and of course, she asked what was wrong and why. I told her that nothing was wrong and that I was doing some research. When she gave me the social, I confirmed that it was her. The site provided me with the last address. As I began to do further research, I learned that after we saw her, she found her way to Baltimore and eventually ended up in a nursing home. My sister did not list anyone for next of kin. I was able to speak to the front desk receptionist and explained why I was calling. She had only good things to say about my sister. How she was always joking and kept everyone laughing. I knew this about her as well. During the times that she was sober, she was enjoyable to be around. She even gave me some advice one day. I recall her telling me how she had avoided being infected by HIV. My sister was telling her baby sister to use condoms. I had received this advice now from three people but never listened. It is only by the grace of

God that I was covered through my escapades. My sister, my mothers' first daughter, had gone into surgery and died from complications. I learned that she had been in the home and a wheelchair for over a year. Before I called my mother back, I called my brother and told him that she was dead. We decided that it was best that I tell mother. When I called, she immediately burst out in tears, but I was able to give my mother some comfort in telling her that for the last two years, she was not on the streets nor using drugs. The state had buried her in an unmarked grave because there was no one listed for them to contact. This may not mean much to you, but my mother had prayed, asking God not to let her daughter die from drugs. Knowing that she was in a safe place, making people laugh and sober let my mother know that although she is not here, God answered her prayers. Of course, this still did not stop her from grieving.

Grief can take many forms and can cause a person to lash out at others. My mother had managed to alienate herself completely from everyone but me, baby girl, and my oldest nephew. As a matter of fact, my niece, the only child that my brother has by his second wife, never got to know my mother and grew up thinking that she was some crazy, mean woman with mental health issues. It's unfortunate because her other grandchildren adored and loved when she would get in the kitchen and throw down, as we called it. My mother could still cook, something that she did exceptionally well. She also was quite the jokester, and I believe this is where my oldest sister got her personality. Her love for entertaining, being surrounded by family and friends remained even after she had given her life to Christ. John 10:10 says that I (Jesus) have come that they might have life and that they may have it more abundantly. It was quite evident that my mother wasn't living an abundant life. How could this be so for someone that was so sold out and had dedicated her life to Christ? Listen, God never said that we had to stop living our life. My mother wanted this for me but was bound herself. We both needed to be free.

By this time, I had started a Master in Business Administration (MBA) with an international focus. I was busy with my course work, baby girls' activities in school, and working a demanding full-time job with the Federal Government. Nevertheless, I still attended church. I was driving 1 to 1 ½ hour, 3 to four times a week. Toward the end of one class, I was pulling a late-night and had to take Baby Girl with me. As a result, I missed the bible study for two weeks. The next Saturday was the usual day when Baby Girl would be in Pasadena for cheerleading practice. That morning I drove Baby Girl to Pasadena MD for practice, and when we arrived, it was dark. I called my brother's wife to learn after wasting time and gas for that matter that the practice had been canceled.

The next day the conversation continued with me calling her about the practice being canceled and no one telling me with her response being, "If you had been at church, you would have known." "Are you serious", I asked? "How about I was working on trying to complete my MBA and doing assignment into the early mornings." Well, she couldn't relate to this, nor did she care about this, remember she was the one that had found a night school for me to attend when I found myself pregnant. I had hopes, dreams, and aspirations that had been delayed for ten years while I dated Mr. Producer. If you want to do better, you must do better. I was focused and determined. The conversation between my brother's wife and I was very disappointing and ugly. She went on to remind me again how I was ungrateful, how she helped me, and that I continue to give her my ass to kiss. My response to her was, "If I am giving you my ass to kiss, then eat my shit, bitch." God was not in this conversation at all, and today, I would not have responded to her in this manner. I left the church after this, and now my relationship with my brother and his wife was estranged. My brother never put my mother and me first. I know that he is supposed to place his family first, and I don't disagree, but what he never stood up as a man to try to mitigate the conflicts that continue to arise.

While working on my MBA, I met someone very different than anyone that I had ever dated. He was helping me with my assignments. When I finally agreed to let him take me out, he showed up at my door with beautiful roses. I put a lot of effort into this date, and even Baby Girl helped me pick out my outfit. She hated shopping with me and said that we would spend hours and hours in the mall and sometimes in one store that she never wanted to visit again. This time she was just as excited as I was to go on an actual date, and he wasn't hook-up. Mr. MBA was interested in more than my body and looks, he recognized that there was more to me and that I had a brain. If you recall, when I was in elementary school, I was the one that would receive all the awards. My academics continued to follow me throughout my life, and I would later lead others as I continued to excel. Mr. MBA didn't miss anything on our date. We took a road trip Philadelphia, and he had purchased VIP tickets to Cirque Du Soleil. We enjoyed the cocktail hour, and the show was terrific. After he took me to dinner, and we ordered everything on the menu. He was a man after my own heart.

Mr. MBA was there to stay, and we had a whirlwind dating experience. He came over one evening and cooked dinner for Baby Girl and me. Then he took me on a date where we sat court-side at the Wizards game. Although this part of my life seemed to be coming together, other parts were falling apart. My mother's health had declined. She was severely diabetic but refused to eat right. If I wasn't taking her candy, my brother was. My mother lived less than a mile from my brother's house, so she would call him more frequently than she would call me. I think it was out of respect that I was in school. She wanted to see me graduate and obtain, yet another degree. I was her pride and joy when it came to my accomplishments.

We had a scare as my mother wasn't answering the phone and we later found out that she had fallen and couldn't get up. She had been lying there for a day. After that, she found a home where a lady was taking care of the elderly and signed herself in. I had been so self-absorbed that I didn't find out until after. Take it from me; you cannot go back in time, so do what's right today. You don't want to live with the life regrets that I have.

When my mother moved in, she sold her car and some of her furniture. While at the house, she was heavily medicated, and it didn't seem like she even existed anymore. It was as if she stared out into space. I had promised to take her out one day but had also decided to purchase a new vehicle on this day. It took so long that I no longer had time to take her out. Again, I was self-absorbed and selfish. Facing the ugly truth, while I write this book, is one of the most difficult things that I have had to do. As I recall that day, she had been dressed, sitting in a chair and waiting for me all day. What kind of person was I? This was my mother! I'm sure that I also contributed to her depression and increased the rejection that she was feeling. While staying at the house, my mother went to get water in the middle of the night and fell. My mother broke her arm when she fell and was rushed to the hospital. It was downhill from here. She never left the hospital. That's right; she went from having a broken arm to having several tests run, to being medically trached. They even wanted to put a feeding tube in her. When a hospital finds out that you have excellent health insurance, this is what happens. Can you imagine going into the hospital for a broken arm and never coming out? That should have never happened. I took Mr. MBA with me one day after class when I went to visit her, and she was in a terrible state. Her eyes were blood red, and her hands were drawn tight as if she had a stroke. Mr. MBA had worked in the health industry for some time and asked if he could read her labs. I found out from him, not the doctors, that my mother had contradicted a bacterial infection from the hospital. Okay, you may think, that happens a lot. You are correct, but the infection was very severe, and she was allergic to penicillin, which made it difficult to treat. My mother was on her death bed.

While working from home one day, I called to get a status update from the nurse and learned that the doctors decided that they needed to put a stint in her heart. I immediately asked who authorized that, they had been calling my brother but was unable to get in touch with him. I am not surprised; every year, my brother takes his family to Orlando for vacation, and this year would not be any different. Everyone had their own lives, and who am I to expect anyone to make changes. I thought that they would have postponed their annual trip this year since a hurricane had recently passed through, leaving most of Orlando without power. Well, I was wrong. I rushed to the hospital to stop them from performing yet another surgery on my mother. When I arrived, she had already been prepped and was in the surgery room. I could care less, and I asked to speak to the surgeon. The surgeon indicated that her heart was fragile and how she needed this surgery as preventive care. What was I supposed to do? I wasn't a doctor, so I told them to go ahead. Having any surgical procedure at this hospital was concerning. My mother contracted the bacterial infection when the hospital tried to give her a colonoscopy. This procedure requires that the patient be prepped before the procedure. Well, the hospital failed to prep, my Mother. She was in the process of having the procedure done when they learned that she had not been prepped, and as a result, fecal matter leaked into her bloodstream from torn tissue. I know you're thinking, you better sue that hospital! Well, I will tell you about that a little later.

It seemed like months went by, and she wasn't getting better. Then when she became coherent again, meaning she recognized that she had visitors, but could not talk. For the last months of her life, she was unable to speak. I believed the hospital also damaged her voice box when they trached her. When visiting one day, I was looking through a wedding magazine and asking her what she thought, and out of nowhere, she just began to cry. She was weeping with sadness; I could see it in her eyes. The last thing that I wanted to do was to make her hurt any more than she already was. Then my Mother started pressing the nurses' button. When the nurse arrived, she began to motion that she wanted me to leave. So, I gathered my belongings and left. That day I was in tears, I could barely walk back to my car. What had I done wrong? Was it something that I said because surely it wasn't the pictures from the magazine? It wasn't as if she had met Mr. MBA or if I had a ring on my finger.

The next day when I returned, she was sedated, so I sat by her bedside and worked. After nearly a week, she started to come around again, and it seemed like she was finally getting better. Mr. MBA had planned a getaway for the two of us, but I didn't want to leave her side. When speaking to my oldest brother he told me that I should go, so I did. We spent an amazing week away at the Ritz Carlton in Jamaica. This was my first time traveling to Jamaica, although I had been to Cancun six times already. It seemed that Mr. MBA was doing everything right. He paid very close attention to every detail of our relationship. The first time that I ever stayed at his house, he had invited me over, and when I arrived, there was a note on the door that said come in.

When I opened the door, there were candles and a note that led to the balcony where a table fully covered with white linen and set for two. On my plate there was a box and a card that said open me. In the box was a beautiful pair of pearls earrings. Then he came around the corner, with the first course. Mr. MBA was an excellent cook; I later found out that he had worked at a 5-star restaurant while in college. The dinner was amazing and at the end he gave me another box. Was he about to ask me to marry him? The look on my face I'm sure was priceless. Well, it wasn't an engagement ring, but it was the most beautiful ring that I had ever seen. It had diamonds and a blue center stone. I was never sure why blue, but it took me nearly ten years for me to realize that blue was my favorite color. Then it happened, I had taken my time getting to know him and listened to my Mother finally who would say stop sleeping with these men so quickly. I had made him wait, and it was completely worth it.

After we returned from the trip, I had gone to sleep on the couch because he snored terribly. This is when I had the dream. In the dream, it was like I was in New Orleans, and the streets were filled with people. They were all dancing, singing, and the band was playing when the saints go marching in. Walking beside me was my mother, my daughter, and my half-sister. In the dream, I turned to my Mother and said, "See, I knew that you were going to get better," with excitement. After waking up and getting dressed, I gathered the troops. I took my daughter and my youngest nephew that had been raised by my Mother to the hospital.

So much had happened in the lives of my sister, who was murdered, sons. After moving to Maryland and staying with my brother, after two years of living in the basement, the oldest of the two went to live with relatives in Silver Springs, Maryland. He was tired of continually having to do all the chores and feeling like he and his brother were being treated differently. They did all the chores and watched while my brothers' wife's daughter who was the same age as the oldest son, did nothing. The oldest of my sister's sons had gone to visit with these relatives a few times, until they finally took him in, leaving his youngest brother behind. Little did we know that would be the last time his little brother would ever see him again. This story takes many turns for the worst. While he was living in Silver Springs, he started to experiment with drugs to the point that he began to get in trouble in school. He was headed down the wrong path; he was born a drug-addicted baby, and we didn't want him to fall into the same trap. Unfortunately, this generational curse had found my baby. I reference him as my baby because when he first came to live with us before I had my own child, he was my responsibility.

While living in Silver Springs, he would visit my Mother from time to time. Then one day our relatives went out of town and left him home alone. He decided that he would take one of their cars for a joy ride, and when returning to the house, hit another one of their vehicles parked in the driveway. That was it for him, and they brought him back to my brothers. When they arrived, guess who opened the door. Exactly, my brother's wife who decided that he could not come in the house because my brother was not home and left him on the porch. Feeling rejected, he left and went to a friend's house nearby. By now, I knew, and my Mother knew what was happening. After talking to him on the phone, he was very strong-minded for a 14-year-old, we were able to convince him to come to my mother's house. For the next few months, we put him on the metro daily to go to school in Silver Spring, but he wasn't telling me that he didn't have enough on his metro card to get there, so he was missing school. After getting into a fight in school, he skipped the next day and was picked up by a truancy officer. When questioned, the social services and the state got involved. He was never allowed to come back to my mothers. The state of Maryland determined that no one had legal custody of him and placed him into a group home. My brother nor his wife got involved; they stayed away. The time at the group home seemed like forever but was very short-lived when we got a call that he had been arrested. He was arrested on the weekend that he promised to visit my Mother. The charges were rape, assault, and burglary. What had he gotten himself into? When I was able to talk with him, and his court-appointed attorney. I learned that he had started dating this girl while at the group home and selling drugs. He was trying to find a way to meet ends without asking anyone for help. He had no mother and never knew who his father was. While visiting his girlfriend, her brother asked if he wanted to go meet up with a couple of his friends and smoke, which meant to get high. He agreed, and this is when is life ended as he would know it. The last day that he would see outside of a prison. He was now 15 years old and at this house was a 14-year-old and his girlfriend's brother, who was also 15. He told me that after they had been drinking and smoking in a vacant ground-level apartment. Out of nowhere, there was knocking at the patio sliding doors. In fear, both he and the 14-year-old jumped back, but his girlfriend's brother knew the guys at the door who were 17 and 18 years old. The problem is that they had a young 15-year-old white girl with them.

They all continued to drink and get high, including the girl that they brought with them. He said that it didn't seem that anything was wrong; he started to feel sick and went outside, threw-up, and smoked a cigarette. When he came back inside the apartment, he said that there was scuffling in the bathroom. So, he went to see what was going on and the guys started to yell at him to get the fuck back! He didn't know these guys, so he and 14-year-old took off running, but getting down the street, my nephew remembered that he had left his jacket that had the drugs in it and went back. If he had only kept going, but he didn't.

After returning to the apartment, he said that it was silent, so he started to walk around. He found everyone in the back room standing in a circle, and the young girl was going around giving everyone head or oral sex, unforced it seemed, but we would never know what led up to this because he was not in the house, although when she got to him, he also allowed her to give him head. Then they all went back into the living room and started to smoke and get high again until the two oldest guys said, "Fuck this we want some pussy." Pardon my language... This was when my nephew said that the girl said no. According to him, he wasn't sober enough to realize everything that was happening. In addition to the weed and alcohol, he was also under the influence of prescription medicine. After being placed in the home, a regime of medication was resumed by the onsite psychiatrist. The older guys took the girl in the back, raped, sodomized, and beat her up, then left her there with the two other boys; his girlfriend's brother, who he barely knew and the 14-year-old who he had just met. He then said that his girlfriend's brother left him and the 14-year-old because they were trying to help her. Since neither of them were sober enough to think correctly, they never called for help. They tried to find money to get her home but didn't have enough and ultimately left her there.

Later that day, after the girl was found by a janitor, the first one to be picked up by the police was the 14-year-old because he lived in the building. He then told the police about who was there, but we never got to hear his side of the story because he was treated as a juvenile. The fact that this was an election year did not work in his favor. The next one to be picked up was my baby nephew; he was easy to find since he was in a group home. The staff at the group home loved and supported him. They immediately notified my mother, but by the time we got involved, it was too late. He was questioned without an adult being present at 15-years-old and charges were brought against him. Initially, he had pled not guilty to the charges and the attorney that he initially had believed that he would be okay. Midway through the sentencing, the first attorney was pulled into another case and he had to transfer the case to another attorney. The new attorney was a female and seemed to know what she was doing but when he was tried in juvenile court, they decided to try him at 15 years old as an adult. How could they do this to a child who had been under medical treatment since he was born and was too intoxicated and high to make the right decision? According to him, he was also afraid of the two older guys because he didn't know them. After being charged as an adult, when brought to trial, his attorney sat us all in a room and said, "The only thing that he can do is to plead guilty to these charges, and I will get him into the Patuxent institution for six months." The institution would review his mental health for six months, then release him. He indicated that if he continued to plead not guilty, he would spend the rest of his life in jail. My baby nephew was adamant about not pleading guilty because he said that he had not raped her. The robbery charge was from him taking her jacket that he said was the same boys' jacket that he had.

All the moving parts was like a motion picture on fast forward. I was trying to get my life together and stay focus, and now this. I didn't know what to tell him, I was a struggling single mother myself, and it seemed that the attorney had his best interest at heart but no one ever thought about this being an election year and the story was plastered in all of the newspapers and on the news. The papers and the news called it a gang rape, him being part of a gang was far from the truth. He didn't even know the boys, and they were now in a gang. Looking at this today, allows me to see the injustice in justice!

He was tried and agreed to plead guilty as my now elderly mother looked at him with tears in her eyes and begged him to listen to the attorney. What had we done? I testified, along with the staff from the group home, who were all character witnesses of his inability to have made a sound decision to include his psychiatrist. Even the victim read a letter that stated that he never touched her or said a word to her. We thought that we had won, at least to say that he got what we thought would only be a six-month sentence. The boys were all tried separately, and the 14-year-old was the only one tried as a juvenile and spent a year in jail. The other boys who performed the rape received double life sentences, and my nephew was initially sentence to an institution. What we didn't know that was on the other side of the plea was a life sentence in jail.

I keep saying that it was an election year because they had to sentence the boys no matter what. With the election, the governor changed, as well as the laws. The law now said that anyone that had received a life sentence was no longer eligible for this program. My nephew was impacted by this administrative change in the law. They ignored the fact that he had mental health issues; they sent him to the Jessup prison and placed him in maximum security with men that had murdered, and he would never be released. His life as he knew it was over. Even while he was in the institution, he was different. I had never seen my baby nephew like this; his hands were trembling from fear, and he was heavily sedated on medication. They stripped him out of the institution and never provided him with medical care.

While in Jessup, he spent most of his time in solitary confinement, and when he wasn't; like clockwork, my mother would say, "Let's go," and we would go see him. Every month when she did her bills, she also made sure to send him money. During this process, my brother nor his wife ever asked how they could help, nor would they come to court to testify on his behalf. Although my relatives showed up in large numbers, their support didn't help as it painted our family as thugs whereas, my brother being a pastor and I was a college graduate would have demonstrated that he had a healthy support system. We are here now; on the other side of that sentence, where he received a life sentence in prison. You will see by the end of my book 18 years later that he is still in prison.

Back to my mother, after gathering, when we arrived at the hospital, they were getting ready to move my mother to a nursing home. As I began to tell her about my dream, tears started to run down her face. When we left, I felt peace that she was going to be alright. Philippians 4:7 tells us The peace of God, which surpasses all understanding, will guard your hearts and your minds in Christ Jesus. The next day, instead of going directly to the hospital as I would normally have done. I went home to take a nap, but I didn't wake up until midnight when my phone rang. It was my brother.

Little did I know when I was taking the exit to go home instead of going to the hospital, that my mother was going into cardiac arrest. I guess the stint that they said that she needed failed to do what the doctors indicated that it would do, which was another way for them to bill the insurance. Sorry to have digressed, the call from my brother was to come to the hospital. When I arrived, she was no longer coherent; she was dying. If only I had known earlier. The hospital had called my brother's house, and his wife decided since we no longer spoke to wait until my brother got home from bible study to tell him what happened. I guess if I had been at church, I would have known. Well now my

Mother was taking her last breath, and I was standing there watching. Mr. MBA came to the hospital and was there by my side to support me along with my brothers. My next to the oldest brother arrived with his girlfriend. I remember him asking as she was slowly dying how long was this going to take because he had to get back to work.

God why was I born into this life, why this family. I had lost my stepfather and now, my mother. I hadn't seen or spoken to the man that I thought was my father since I was a sophomore in college. God, why? The room cleared as my oldest brother said he was going to step out. I thought he had left. Her heart began to beat slower and slower I began to sing, "I know it was the blood, I know it was the blood," this was the only thing that I knew that had changed my mothers' life. It is so hard for me to write this as I am crying as if it just happened, but I believe that God is healing me. She was gone. My mother had left this world. As I walked out, Mr. MBA had to hold me up, and I recall seeing my brother sitting on the side. No doubt, he was grieving the only way that he knew how. I went home at 4 am and laid down about 4 hours later, something woke me up and I had this unction to call my brother. When I did, I learned that he was already making funeral arrangements. It had only been 4 hours, and he was doing it without me.

I went over to the house, and when he called the insurance company, they asked him who Tonya Alston was, and he replied, "That is my sister." They then explained to him that my mother had changed her beneficiary over to me and that I needed to make the decisions. When I got on the phone, I told them that I would get back in touch with them. My brother had also called his Pastor and arranged to have the funeral there. My Mother never attended that church and didn't care for this Pastor, but he thought that was where the service should be held. Because I wasn't up to arguing, I agreed. The one thing that I could control at this point were the arrangements. So, I decided to go home and told them that I would let them know when I was ready to make the arrangements.

The funeral was held at the church that my brother chose. At the service, it seemed like it was me against my brother, but I'm thankful for those who were close to me for showing their support. We all met at my brothers' house, but we were not together in love. It was a somber time. I had managed to handle the arrangements and getting her body prepared without a problem, but when I walked in the service, my legs went out from under me. But my college roommate was right there to catch me, her and my ex's sister, as well as Mr. MBA. I cried the entire service while my brother sat at the head with his family, again as if he was in charge. The cards that were given to the family all went to my brother, and I was not allowed the opportunity even to read them. When it was over, there were still loose ends to tie up. My brother had told the owner of the home where my Mother was staying that she could keep the tv and the furniture. When I arrived in addition to the tv and the furniture, they had also decided to divide my mother's wardrobe. I didn't have it in me to fight, so I left it all there. What was I going to do with it anyway? Every day on my route home, I had to pass by where my Mother lived before, she signed herself into the home, and I would cry and relive the night of her death repeatedly. One day, I heard a small voice say, " Would you rather have her with you so you can see and touch her, have her sick, depressed and sad or for her to be in a place of peace." After that day, I stopped weeping and would only shed a tear here and there over the next 20 years until now when I started on this journey. I tell you God has his way.

Later my relationship with Mr. MBA took a turn, and my heart had gotten hardened not only from bad relationships but now with the addition to the loss of my Mother. I didn't want to be bothered. My mother was gone, the hospital had killed her, and my family was divided. I started to treat Mr. MBA mean on purpose to push him away. The one that stood by my side, holding my hand until my Mother took her last breath and held me up at the end. Later, when I was at his house, I found a receipt where he had purchased an engagement ring. I never told him that I knew, but I wasn't ready. I was so broken inside that I just pushed him away, and four months later, it was over. He tried so hard to make it work, and I live with the regrets even today as I now see that he has gotten married, obtained his PhD, and is very successful. I'm sure he is an amazing husband and father if he treated her anything close to how he had treated me. We would graduate soon; I finished the MBA program, but my Mother wasn't there to see it.

My graduation day, which was now only eight months after losing my Mother, was bittersweet. It had been Baby Girl and me against the world. Although we were pursuing legal action against the hospital, my brother and I were not on speaking terms. Yes, my mother had made me the beneficiary, but he had her bank card and decided what he was going to do with what was remaining. When I asked about the balance, he indicated that he had given my other brother the rest, who was rushing her to die. Still, despite how he acted, he was one of her children, so I left it alone.

I had invited my oldest brother to my graduation, and Baby Girl was starting work that day. She had obtained a worker's permit and was staring her first day as the character Tweety-Bird at Six Flags. She was so sad that I was making her go to work instead of attending my graduation, but I was trying to teach her to have integrity. After dropping her off, I was alone and almost didn't go to the graduation. Mr. MBA wasn't there either. Had I hurt him that bad that he didn't come because he didn't want to see me. He was graduating and was practically the reason I was graduating. When I walked across the stage, although there was no one to scream my name, I knew that my mother was proud. I remembered the day that I had applied, and they told me that I needed to pay a $500 registration fee that I didn't have. Just when I was going to give up, my mother gave me the money, and in my heart, I felt proud to walk across that stage for her. I later found out that although my brother didn't attend my graduation that he decided to attend graduation for one of his church members, held at the same location later that day.

Chapter 17

Black Hearted

After being used and taken advantage of in relationships by men, supposed friends, and family, my heart had grown to be hard and dark. I didn't care about anyone at this point, but Baby Girl. Consequently, my new attitude was that I was going to get mine, and I didn't care who I hurt while doing it. There had been so many other men from NFL to NBA players, the entertainment industry to include rappers and an R&B artist who begged for my company. Most women would think that I was crazy after seeing him naked with only cornrows, but something wasn't right, and I decided to pass. I only cared about getting what I wanted and would use them for their money, gifts, sex, or whatever I wanted at that time. I could easily have sex with a man and then tell him, okay, you can leave now. Neither the Church nor God was in my thoughts. It was as if I had never believed. That I had forgotten about my friend that was there with me as a child, I could never really put my finger on how it was possible to be so separated from God, although I know now that God was never separate from me. We often leave God, but Deuteronomy 31:6 tells us that he will never leave nor forsake us.

About a year after my mother passed, I had a meeting with a couple of men that wanted to talk to me about how to obtain government contracts. The meeting went so well that I looked at the owner of the company as my next target. He was charming, too kind, and I could see that he was gullible. From the moment that I laid eyes on him; I was determined to turn him out. If you are wondering what that means, I was determined to get all that I could get out of him. It all happened so quickly. When we first met, he did not have on a ring, but I later learned that he was married with two young children, a boy, and a girl, but I didn't care. It was clear that I was working my way down the list of ten commandments. Thou shall NOT commit Adultery was next. I had already broken; thou shall NOT steal; my closet was full. I had an excess of clothes from my days in retail. I had even figured out that if someone had a large cash purchase that I could easily do a return and pocket the cash. Now I was a thief, how about thou shall not steal? I wasn't supposed to be this weak. I was supposed to be strong. When I was in college, my great aunt, the Pastor, died. After the funeral, while sitting in the car at the gravesite with my brother, I recall him asking me if I had ever received the gift of the holy ghost. The topic came up because we were discussing my struggles, but I didn't think that was possible, I was far from even trying to live right. At the funeral, I was reminded of my past relationship with God. He then explained that the Holy Ghost was a helper to strengthen me when I was weak. Based on how I was taught growing up, according to the Pentecostal criteria to be filled with the Holy Ghost or the fire baptism of God with the evidence of speaking in tongues required that you tarry as they called it, before God and live a sanctified life. Then it happened. My brother asked me a question, and he said, "If your daughter was hungry, would you give her food to eat, and I said yes." He explained that was all that was required was for me to ask for it. Then God decides when you're ready to be filled with his spirit. Suddenly, while tears flowed from eyes and I begin to thank God, tongues of fire flowed like a river nonstop. It wasn't like a babble that I often hear today when others are filled; it was as if it was there all along and just waiting to be made known. I was told that this power would help me to live right, so why wasn't I living right. What I know is that God will not get in the way of our choices. Just like Adam and Eve, they chose to disobey God. I chose to disobey him, as well. It was clear that I lived my life based off emotion. I was searching for something that I couldn't find. I was searching for love in all the wrong ways and the wrong places. I was breaking all the ten commandments! Fornicate, well, I can no longer even count the number. I may not have killed anyone physically, but I've definitely murdered a few people with my mouth.

Now back to Mr. Gullible. He was very inexperienced sexually to be someone that was working so hard to be with me. At the start, I told him that it wasn't a good idea at the moment when my conscience kicked in; he was married with two children. According to him, he was not happily married and would tell me that they slept apart. As time went on, I discovered that he had his own set of issues. While some people are addicted to porn, he, on the other hand, spent a lot of time in massage parlors. He wasn't the porn type but preferred his women to be submissive. I was far from submissive, and soon I made him mine. I now know that I was working under a Jezebel spirit. A spirit of manipulation. I would do things to him that I knew he had never experienced before. Besides, I had never had just one boyfriend I would always make sure that I had at least three. It was as if I needed each of them for different reasons. It was easy for me to treat him this way because, for me, it was only sex. I wasn't even sure if my heart would allow me to love anyone ever again. I was too broken. I had also allowed myself to date someone who I thought was an ordinary guy. It wasn't anything special about this one; he wasn't an athlete, he wasn't in the entertainment industry, and yet, he still managed to make me regret the day that I allowed him into my heart. I found myself driving by where he lived to see if he was there and if he was lying to me. I was mostly correct to follow my instinct; he was a habitual liar. He had a longtime girlfriend that he never told me about and another girl that he had seen for years. Where did I fit into all of this? That's right; I was just someone that he used. He was a short guy, and his claim to fame was that he would play on local football teams. I attended a couple of the games and saw the longtime girlfriend from afar. I didn't know about her until that day. It was embarrassing because everyone knew but me. I believed he told her that I was with one of the other guys and not him, but later we both talked. We planned to set him up one day when he was over my house. I was going to leave the door unlocked so that she could catch him, but she decided against it and to believe his lies. I decided to move on!

Meantime, I was sneaking around with Mr. Gullible from hotel to hotel. Not once did I think about his wife or what I was doing to his marriage. He wanted to spend time with me so badly that he would drive nearly two hours to get to my house just to have sex with me. It didn't take long, he couldn't get enough of me, and I planned to get out of him exactly what I wanted. I soon had him paying me monthly to work for his company. I started hosting meetings with his team and soon had a significant role in his business. When we met, his company was failing, and he only had three employees left. I managed to help him get his company back on track. He had won a new contract and would soon win others. One night while being at the office late working on a proposal, I called and sent a text when I arrived home and used the word babe in the message. What I quickly learned was that the text had been intercepted by his wife, and she had gotten angry and left the house. She was finished with his escapades. I wasn't the first woman that she had caught him with, and this time would be the last time that he would cheat on her. She left him and didn't look back. He called me immediately, upset, of course, but I felt like he needed me now more than ever. I had never been married and ran from the idea when I found the receipt for the engagement ring that Mr. MBA was going to give me. What did I know about the sanctity of marriage? Besides, my heart was so black; I only cared about what made me happy. Baby Girl despised him and would tell me regularly how she didn't like him and felt that he didn't like her. Mr. Gullible was a needy man and would get upset if anyone was getting more attention than him. We would often disagree; he believed that Baby Girl was spoiled.

I recall one day when we were together, the tables of my heart turning towards him. Sex, for me, was no longer passionate. I set pleasure goals to make him not want to ever be without me. One day, during the act, he looked me in my eyes and put his fingers over his lips as in to say quiet. The dynamics of our relationship changed this day, and I opened my heart.

I opened my heart and saw a real opportunity with him. I threw myself into the company with him, and we spent time picking out furniture for the new house. We spent multiple days a week together, either I was at his home, or he was at mine. He loved my cooking, something that I never even had the opportunity to do for Mr. Producer. When we were not eating out, I was making his favorite meal. I had figured out all his pleasure points. We were a couple, at least that is what I thought. A couple of years had passed now, and he was officially divorced. He and his ex-wife would have shared custody, and he managed to protect the children throughout this process. I met them once early on before the divorce. He had them with him in the car. His daughter was about three and needed her hair combed, and I did her hair. When it was time for him to leave, she cried and didn't want to leave me. I believe he realized that was a mistake because it never happened again.

As time went on, I caught him cheating a few times. The sad thing is that he wasn't very good at cheating. He even introduced me to one of the women that he was seeing. One Christmas, when I was at the house, something told me to go downstairs and to look in the back bedroom. I wasn't sure why because this room was not occupied and was one of three guest rooms in the basement. In that room behind the closet door was a shopping bag. He had purchased another woman the same gifts for Christmas that he had bought for me. I was enraged but thankful that I found the items. I left the house, and when he called, I did not answer. That night, I finally responded to his texts and confronted him. He lied and told me that he bought the items for his mother. Did he think that I believed that he had bought his 60-year-old mother a short satin pink robe, with a glitter butterfly on the back from Victoria Secret? That was all I needed, and my heart was black again. From that moment on, I never felt the same way about him. This time I was not only hurt, but I was angry. I had allowed myself to love him more in-depth than I had ever loved anyone else. It seemed to be real, and we did all the things that someone in a normal healthy relationship would do. Once this happened, I saw him; differently but did not let go.

Chapter 18

She's Not Going to Make It

The year is 2009, and we have our first African American President. I was still hanging on to what I thought was the deepest love of my life. I had applied to be detailed out of the current Section, where I worked and was approved. The detail was to work at the White House and run acquisitions under the new administration. What a fantastic opportunity to work under the first African American President, I was honored and excited but would never make it there. On July 4th, after spending the weekend in our newly furnished and custom painted home, I returned to my place in Alexandria, Virginia. I had been battling a headache for a week that started to feel like a toothache.

The dentist believed that I was grinding my teeth in my sleep and figured he would sand my teeth down. Two days later, after getting back home. I told Baby Girl that I was going to pick up seafood for later because I was going to hang out with some friends for the 4th of July. Well, I never made it to the party, and I never made it to my detail at the White House. I left the grocery store in an ambulance. I called Baby Girl to tell her what was going on and where to pick up the

149

truck. The next thing that I knew, I woke up after being in a coma and hospitalized for 30 days. I had a seizure in the grocery store and was found in an aisle. When I arrived at the hospital, according to Baby Girl they gave me a CT scan and said that they saw something but wasn't sure what it was. It was enough that they kept me in the hospital. I'm sure you think well that was good when actuality it was and wasn't at the same time. Since it was a holiday weekend, the hospital was short-staffed, and as a result, I laid in a bed and deteriorated for thirteen hours. Baby Girl watched me as I could no longer use my left side, and my face grew numb. I had a stroke while in the hospital. The doctors nor nurses even knew what was going on until Baby Girl said that she lost it, no longer being able to control her anger and demanded that they come and see about me.

I was given a second scan, and this time, what they thought was nothing was a blood clot that had now burst and was bleeding out. Yes, my brain was swelling, and at 4:00 am. the doctor told Baby Girl, "There is nothing else that we can do; she is going to die." Can you imagine not having a father in your life, your grandmother has passed and now all you have left in the world besides your dog can be the next one to go? When she tells this story, I can't stop fighting back the tears. She was a freshman in college and had the weight of the world on her shoulders. She told me that she called Mr. Gullible and although he was concerned it was his week with the children, so he didn't come to the hospital. God had to be there with Baby Girl as she had me medevacked to another hospital where they housed top neurologists. While I was there, my condition was so critical that they placed me in a seduced comma. I was told that even the sound of people's voices would raise my blood pressure to a vital state. Baby Girl sat by my side day and night.

Before my mom passed while I worked in retail, God blessed me with a woman who adopted me as her own. I never knew that one day she would take on the role of being a mother in my life. Her and her husband, who I fondly refer to as Mom and Dad took their part in me and Baby Girl's life seriously; they never missed a birthday, dance recital, nor holiday. When my own family wasn't there, they were always by our side. Even now, while I was in the hospital when no one knew what the outcome would be, they were there. God knew what was to come with me losing my mother and now facing death myself; we needed them now more than ever. The blessed part about this is that no one can tell her that she is not my mom! I have tenderly accepted my blessing in her, the gift from God to be able to call her mom. Mom and Dad are extraordinary. I had never met anyone as giving and loving as the two of them. Having been married now almost 30 years, they set an example for me that I hope to one day have.

By my side were also my Diva Girls as we called ourselves. I met these wonderful women while working at the Department of Justice. There was no stopping us, and we did everything together from shopping to lunch. My Diva Girls taught me how to laugh and love myself. We met during a transitional time for me after losing my mom. We talked about my dating, and they made me realize that I didn't need to have three at a time, so I began to settle with who I called Mr. Gullible. Before getting sick, he wasn't that to me anymore. He was a man that I adored more than Mr. Producer, who I thought would be my forever true love. This time I felt like he was everything that I needed and that we would happily be together forever. My Diva Girls were there. I was closet to ReeRee, she was more than just a Diva Girl; she became a sister to me, a best friend. Everyone loved her; she could sing and was the life of the party, but deep down, she didn't know how much she was loved. She truly adored Baby Girl and became like an aunt to her, so much so that I found out later than during Sunday brunch she would sneak her mimosas. I know it was only with love and that she would never do anything to harm her. As I write this, I realize how much I miss her, as a few years after my health scare, she was found dead in her home. My heart still aches for my friend.

Time for me was passing fast, and today was the day when they would take me off life-support. Baby Girl said that she had gone out to the truck and had a talk with God. In the conversation, she said that she made him some promises. When she came back in and as they took me off life-support, they say that my eyes and mouth were in two different directions, and while they sat and watched, God worked a miracle my face slowly came back together. After more time had passed and I realized that I was in the hospital, I was paralyzed on my left side and was in a diaper. The 5'5 woman that stood more like 5'8 walking in 5-inch heels couldn't walk at all, and when I looked in the mirror, I saw an old woman. I didn't know what would become of me.

As I remained in the hospital after being transferred to three different facilities, I was finally in a place that cared. It was time for my rehabilitation. This facility was determined to get me back to a state where I could do for myself. The one prior would have kept me in a vegetative state. Since I was in a diaper, when I needed to use the bathroom, it required assistance. The nurse assigned, told me that she wasn't going to keep hurting her back to take me to the bathroom, and one day I sat in a saturate diaper for four hours. When Baby Girl arrived, she was furious and notified the head of the hospital's administration, and before I knew what was happening, I was moved to another location. I had no idea that she had all this strength. Growing up with a single mother, I guess, required her to know more about life than other young girls her age. As the word got around, more people began to come. My college roommate, who was now married and had a combined family of eight, found out and was on her way. She arrived with her entire family asking what you need me to do. She wasn't just a roommate; God had given me a sister. I had lost both of my biological sisters, but God foreshadowed what was to come in my life. "What do you need," she asked, and what I wanted more than anything was a bath. The hospital had wiped me down with a cloth for over a month. I wanted to feel the warm water on my body, and a bath is what I got. I don't know how she does what she does, but this woman is strong and has self-esteem that would outshine the brightest star. She believes that she can do anything and proves it to people every day. From growing up bullied to becoming a model and owning multiple businesses. She is now raising a blended family, to include one with autism. She is a phenomenal woman to me who was humble enough to wash every nook and cranny of my body. Now that is love and friendship that will never go away. She also called my original hairstylist from when I was in college and told her what happened. She now lived in New York styling for the stars. Who would have thought that she would have taken the time for me, but one day while I sat in the wheelchair, there she was with a yellow rose and her styling bag. She had driven four hours from New York to do my hair. My old roommate knew what I needed to boost my self-esteem. It didn't get me out of the wheelchair, but it helped with how I saw myself in the mirror.

Mr. Gullible would come by but not as much as he should have. This only separated him and Baby Girl more. She did not feel like he was there. I would have thought that he would have made sure that she had food to eat and an opportunity to go home from time to time, but he didn't. Baby Girl explained how it was the women from my MBA program, the Diva Girls and Mom that looked out for her.

For me, every day was a new day of learning. My brain had to reprogram itself. There I was a woman with an MBA who couldn't draw a clock, and I repeatedly asked about my detail to the White House. Baby Girl had to tell me again and again that I never made it there, but I still had hope. It had taken me six months to get approval for the detail, and now three months had passed. Although I was going through my top-secret clearance, they couldn't continue to hold the spot open for me. I had to face the fact that it wasn't going to happen, but it only made me more determined to walk again.

Rehabbing and being potty trained as a child were different levels of difficulties that I had to endure. Baby Girl was there, pushing me even when it felt like I was lifting a ton every time I tried to move my left side. One of the nurses there pushed me as well and told me that if I didn't get out of the diaper that they would send me to a nursing home. She then brought me a pair of hospital panties. From that day forward, I had to learn to train my bladder. I have so much empathy for little children now having had to experience this as an adult. One night, about three in the morning, I could no longer hold it and wet the bed. I tried to roll over, but because I could not use my left side, and the night nurse would not come when called, I laid there in the urine all night. This time in my life was very humbling. I had to ask for baths, help to the bathroom, and even Mr. Gullible had to wipe me once after a bowel movement. I should have known then that it was over after seeing the look on his face. The doctors didn't have much hope in me learning to walk again. People that I didn't know that cared continued to show up to visit. Even Mr. Freshmeat came to visit me in the hospital standing by my bedside, hoping that I would get better.

He had relocated from North Carolina with his family. He and his wife had an on again off again relationship; they both seemed to cheat on each other. One great thing about him was that he was a provider and would work multiple jobs with little sleep, continually trying to earn money. His wife was an attorney, and when they relocated, he left a long-term career and had been unable to find another one. Over the years, we had stayed in touch and would hook-up from time to time when I would return to North Carolina for homecoming. By now, she knew me, but I honestly could care less. I felt that he never wanted to marry her but was too afraid to call the wedding off the night before. My thoughts were foolish as I know now, but then that is how I felt in my heart. Today, we are friends with no physical connection, for me anyway.

Nonetheless, he visited, and a couple of other guys who I was only friends with did as well until Mr. Gullible caught a severe attitude. He requested that the hospital ward place a sign-in sheet at the nurses' station for anyone that wanted to visit me. He was trying to keep track of who was there when he wasn't, which is funny because who was keeping track of him.

Soon I learned to walk again. I remember the day that I took my first steps; I was like a little child. The doctors decided that, well, she might walk, but she will never walk in heels again. Little did they know the God that I once sat and talked to was still in control of it all. The day that I was released from the hospital, I went directly to the nail salon and the mall. I needed to buy flat shoes because all the shoes that I owned were 4 inches or higher. I spent $1000 that day on flat shoes but never wore one pair of them. While at home for another three months, I would walk around the house in my heels, trying to regain the strength in my legs. I never knew that walking in heels required that I lift my body weight, no wonder so many women would ask how do you walk in those. Looking at me on the outside, I am judged by the way that I dress or present myself. My investment in shoes after learning to walk in heels again would keep heads turning. When given the opportunity, I always tell women as I walk around in my 5-inch red bottoms that you might wear my size, but you would never be able to wear my shoes. I will save this for another book but walking in my shoes would take years of abuse, hurt, pain, and recovery. I'm not sure how many women could face what I have encountered in my life.

Every day I worked on getting better and was taking several different types of medications. For someone that had never been sick before, it started to weigh on me. Every week I had my blood drawn because of the number of blood thinners that I had to take daily. My arms were black and blue from the needles. My left arm seemed to have a permanent mark that looked like a tattoo that covered the circumference from having had a blood pressure cuff tightly around my arms for over a month. My murmuring started to upset Baby Girl because she was the one that had been with me every day through all of this. One day she said, "Mommy, please stop! You have no idea what I have been through, and I made God a promise that if he healed you that I would never complain again." I watched and listened as she described the events that surrounded my near-death experience with tears in her eyes. Wow! I had no idea just how close to death I had been. She also explained how Mr. Gullible wasn't there for her; he would come by but never really spent time there with me. Others that I thought were helping Baby Girl, I later learned, was a burden, like my youngest nephew that was raised as my little brother. After running away from my brothers nearly two years after his older brother, he left in the middle of the winter with snow on the ground, and might I add with no coat; he had become a wanderer going from place to place with a backpack. Being there with Baby Girl required that she not only had to feed herself, but now she was feeding him, her older cousin or uncle.

Over the years, he lived with me from time to time, but I would always have to ask him to leave for one reason or another. He would refuse to bath on a regular basis or keep a job, and I was not the type to have a grown man just laying around doing nothing. Now I realize that he was misunderstood. Not ever knowing his mother because she was murdered not long after he was born, nor did he know his father and his uncle that he loved only disciplined him. Having these issues, what else could he do but wander to different places as he tried to find his way. It's taken years, but I am happy to say that after two children and a slight jail sentence, he now seems to have discovered what it is meant to be a man and a father. He has a job with the DC government, an apartment that he can call home, that no one can put him out of unless the bills don't get paid, and I am proud to say that he has custody of his daughter and son. I find it interesting as I sit back and watch him tell the children that it is nap time. This man was there all along dormant, and I am so thankful to God because things could have gone an entirely different way. His older brother remains in prison with no notion of a release.

Chapter 19

Shattered Heart

Being at home and not back to work only gave me more time to focus on Mr. Gullible. One morning about 4:00 am, I woke up, and something told me to log into my emails. The day before, Mr. Gullible used my laptop to log into his email. What I found when I logged in was that all his emails had downloaded into mine. I searched the email for keywords like love, and after two hours, I found nothing. I gave up and felt that my instinct had been wrong, but I could not go back to sleep. I had to keep looking; it was a strong pull that something wasn't right. After going back into the email, this time, I searched on sex and investigated the deleted folder. In that folder I found was my instinct had been drawing me too. There were a series of emails between him another woman. The emails asked her when was the last time she had been tested, and she responded that she had just had an OBGYN appointment, but he wanted to know if she had taken the real test. At this point, it was clear to me that either they had already had sex, or they were planning to have sex. One thing about Mr. Gullible is that he was going to be safe. This was a good thing for me, given my shaded past relationships. I quickly learned through the deleted emails that this was the same woman that he had purchased the satin robe for that he lied and told me was for his mother. It was still going on. He had been seeing her long before I had gotten sick, and while I was in the hospital, their relationship had gotten more serious.

On this same day, I was scheduled to be on a conference call with his team. Now, although I had not returned to my job, I was already supporting him again. I will say that through it all, he continued to pay me while I was in the hospital. Maybe he wasn't the gullible one, I was. I was the one that had stood on the sidelines and dated him while he was married. Thou Shall Not Commit Adultery, well I did that too, and look at what happened. Karma is real, and now it is happening to me.

While on the call, he would text me like normal with his sweet morning gestures, but this time I wasn't interested in what he had to say. I text him that someone that I knew told me that he was seeing one of my friend's line sisters. Go figure this girl was a Delta. It must be something about them and me. I was rejected by the sorority, but Mr. Freshmeat married one, and Mr. Gullible is now cheating on me with one. I looked her up on a professional social media network and found her picture. When I saw her, I realized that I had met her before. One evening, he was headed out to meet his partner in the company, and I decided that I would go too. Even though he knew that I was coming, he had also invited his side girl as well. I met them at a bar in DC that he only knew about because of me, and she joined later. He pretended that she was there for his business partner and was the one that was helping them at the bank.

It is all so clear to me now. Not only was Mr. Gullible seeing someone else, but to flaunt her in my face was a first and unforgivable. How disrespectful can you be?! Out of the awful relationships that I had been in, this was one thing that had not happened. I had known her all along. After the conference call ended, he called, and

I confronted him to a point where he could no longer lie to me. He didn't think that I would fully recover from the stroke, and besides I wasn't the glamourous beauty that he had dated, I was the one that disgusted him as I remember the look on his face the day that he had to help wipe me. Was this the man that I told God; thank you for allowing me to feel love the way that I had felt it from him. It was clear that I was in some psychological delusion as he managed to talk his way out of yet another situation and make more promises that it wouldn't happen again.

Baby Girl started working at the company while on spring and summer breaks, providing Mr. Gullible administrative assistance. One day while filing items away, she found a check where he had paid the car payment of another woman. When she told me, I decided not to say anything but to wait. Besides, it seemed that we were back on track, at least I was anyway. I was back in my heels and makeup with my normal stride. If I didn't tell you that I had a near-death experience, a brain aneurism that included a stroke, you would never know. There was no residual damage, according to the neurologist and hematologist that had taken an interest in my file. They could not figure out why this happened to me, so they decided to blame it on the birth control, although my blood had no clotting factors and negated this assumed diagnosis.

Another instance occurred where he was determined that he needed to bring someone on board to help with the company accounting. I soon learned that this was a woman of interest as Baby Girl had found a text message on his phone. Yes, it was now a situation where when you look for trouble, you will find it. I was finding it under every rock that I turned over. So, one night after Baby Girl found a receipt for a David Yurman bangle, I had finally had enough. I got dressed, just the way that I knew he would love and showed up at the house. I decided that I wasn't going to call first. I was going to make my presence known. After the first instance, I decided that I needed my own home and not to assume that we would live this long life together. Consequently, I purchased a condo in Arlington, Virginia, that was about 45 minutes from where he was.

When I knocked on the door, he was more than surprised but alone. I didn't catch him, but I confronted him. I told him what I knew and that it was over. He went into a rage, almost as if he was going to attack me. Having experienced this before, I looked him dead in his eyes. In my mind, I thought if he puts his hands on me, I going to kill him! Well, he didn't put his hands on me, but instead, he decided to punch a hole through the door leading downstairs. I quietly got my purse and coat and headed to the front door. I saw a side of him that I hadn't seen before. He met me at the door nearly in tears, saying please don't leave me and immediately I thought this is how he felt when his ex-wife walked out on Valentine's Day. I couldn't do this to him, he was so sad, and besides, I loved this man. So, I stayed, and we made love, more passionate than ever before. That morning, I knew I still needed to leave that I couldn't put myself in another perpetual cycle that was going nowhere fast.

The days after were quiet for us. I even got a new haircut. Looking back now almost ten years, that seemed to be the way that I delivered myself from one man to the next. When I was done with Mr. Producer, and he showed up at the house, I had cut my hair as well. This time, I was determined to do things that I had been putting off in my life. I decided to get braces and take swimming lessons. Although I could swim, I never learned to tread water, which kept me out of the deep end. I also turned my passion for baking into a business and went to take courses that would certify me in the decorating and designing cakes. Soon, I was getting orders for weddings and birthdays. My bakery was called Taste2Love Bakery. While I was keeping myself busy, so was Mr. Gullible. I was giving him more time to develop a new relationship. For Mr. Gullible birthday, I made him a custom cake that looked like DJ turntables, and when he wasn't excited, I knew something was wrong. I could see on the face of the staff when I arrived at his office; they would just look at me. I had become the outsider, we were disconnected, and Baby Girl wasn't working there anymore, she had returned to school.

When I realized what was happening, I decided that I wasn't leaving without a fight. Besides, my hard work helped build this company. I started making demands that he needed to pay me to go, or I would cause him to lose the contracts that he awarded. What drove me to this point was that his niece, who was getting married, after sending me an invitation, told me that I didn't have to come. I was debating anyway and had realized that the relationship that I thought I had built with his sister never really existed. We had initially bonded when it was time to send our daughters away to college. They were both attending the same University, but she was having difficulty with financing. I was able to help her figure out how to get loans to send her daughter to school. I was hopeful that our daughters would have a bond, but they took one look at each other and decided that this was a relationship that would be maintained from afar. None the less, I did not attend the wedding and found out that Mr. Gullible took someone else. He had moved on, so now I was angry with everyone. His sister wasn't answering my calls, and when I asked him if he wanted to work things out, he said no. Then my revenge started! I received a hefty payout to leave. Soon after I left, he and his business partnership were dissolved.

I spent every day going over in my mind how he cheated on me and why. I thought about getting back at him, like destroying his property and poisoning the dog to the point that I decided to have counseling. I was shattered and spent nights in tears that I would never experience again. I was Mrs. Gullible because he had turned the tables on me. After four years, I had opened my hardened heart to what I thought was love only to have it broken in a million pieces. Thankfully this time, I turned to the only thing that had ever given me peace, God.

Chapter 20

Returned but Gone Too Soon

When I was sick, after being placed on life-support, Baby Girl decided that she should call my oldest brother and let him know what was going. From what I learned later; he made a big deal of it to his congregation of how he needed to come to my rescue. My brother and the family went to the hospital to pray for me while I was on life-support. I understand that while they were there, my brother's wife offered Baby Girl a place with them, if I didn't pull through. I am sure that she meant well, but wasn't this the opposite of the prayer? If you are praying and expecting me not to get better, what was the purpose? This disturbed Baby Girl, and she declined because she knew God was going to heal me, and she kept the faith. She also knew the negative impact they had on the lives of both my nephews. Unaware of every incident that happened when I was sick, I started to drive from Virginia to Baltimore, Maryland, to attend his church. I started attending slowly at first because I wasn't sure after how things had ended the first time. Later, I found myself traveling there 4-5 times a week. The trips during the weekday would take 2 hours going in traffic and 1 hour to return, which wasn't healthy for me. Yes, the doctors couldn't find any residual damage, but I was taking an enormous about of medicine. I would get off the shuttle at my place from the metro and get directly into the car without using the bathroom or eating. My brother had explained to me how he needed my help. He and his wife had an incident with another woman at the church, and she was using it against him.

The woman at the church had been a member for some years, and his wife believed she was responsible for her life transformation. My brother's wife would tell me how she had to teach her to dress correctly and did her hair regularly at no charge. This woman spent a lot of time with family, and was often at their home, went out to dinner with them, and on vacations. The relationship between her and my brother had grown as well. My brother had even taken this woman with him to visit their youngest daughter in college. I guess his wife soon caught on because she caught him at her house one day. As I understand it from the woman that went to the church or her side of the story, the brother's wife showed up at her house and cursed her out about her husband; she thought he was there because his van was parked there. She told his wife that he wasn't there, but I learned that he had just gone out the other door. I cannot say that anything ever happened, but I do know that my brother called me one evening and said, "I need to get away, and I told my wife that I was coming to your house." Yes, my brother, the Pastor wanted me to lie to her in case she called. Thankfully she never called, and I didn't have to lie. What I do know is what I felt the day that I saw this woman. It was the second time that I decided to visit his church before going regularly. When I headed to my car after service, I saw the two of them coming from behind the building, and my brother decided to introduce me to her. Something didn't feel right at that moment, but I never said anything.

I'm not sure why I started going back to this church, was it God, or did I want to be around my family. I had enjoyed being away from the family and the drama for three years. It was the best time of my life;

I purchased a home and was making plenty of money. After leaving Mr. Gullible, I took on some other clients that paid me a percent of the contracts that they won. For three years, me and Baby Girl was having the best time of our lives traveling and shopping. She would comment, are we rich? My brother had a situation where he couldn't pay the insurance on the church and asked that I not tell his wife. I gladly supported the need and provided a $1300 check.

Traveling back and forth with no one offering me a place to stay until almost six months later, had taken a toll on me. I decided to rent my house out in Arlington and then rent me a place in Maryland that was about 20 minutes from the church. Relocating, made it easier for me to get to choir practice and support the other administrative roles where I was serving the ministry. Was I doing this for God, or had I been doing all of this for my brother? During this time, while healing from my shattered heart, my relationship with God began to change. I started to seek him in ways that I had not done before. I was hungry for the word and to get in close relations with God. Deep down, I always knew that I would return one day as I had accepted the call to preach the gospel before my mother passed; according to Romans 11:29 For God's gift and his call are irrevocable or without repentance. I was like the prodigal son that had returned home. My brother's wife's daughter oversaw the choir and praise team. She asked me if I could join to help her out. Although my spirit said no, my love for singing said yes. I would later learn to listen to the spirit of God.

I learned a lot after returning to the church and forged some strong friendships as well. I also made several mistakes. Since this was the first family, some people wanted to talk badly about them or to get gossip about them, and unfortunately, I fell into the trap. Being there, I grew spiritually, seeing the gifts of the spirit in operation through me. My brother would call on me often to give a word of knowledge to the church and knew that God had called me to be an evangelist. After a couple of years, God had used me during alter calls to pray for the people and demonstrated his power through me. The spirit of God would always tell me to use my brother's wife when doing the altar call because the people knew her and trusted her spiritually. I was still the new kid on the block. What most people don't realize, and what was demonstrated in biblical times, is that healing requires faith. The fact that they trusted her allowed the spirit to flow more freely. I never shared this with her but allowed her to think it was something God was using her to do directly as people would fall out under the power of God, and I would not even have to touch them. I recall my oldest nephew and my brother coming one day to a conference, and the Power of God was moving and my nephew telling me that women were falling out under the power without even being touched. Again, it is based on faith. It was nothing that I could ever do without God. Surely, this was where God had called me to be.

Unfortunately for me, I had gotten myself caught in a gossip ring. It started with the woman that my brother's wife thought was messing with her husband. The people in this church would engage me in conversation then gossip with the wife or First Lady about only what I said and would never disclose what they were saying. Besides, I loved my family in ways that they even did not understand. Although I was back, there were still walls between us that had not demolished. One day my brother's wife and his youngest daughter were out near my house. I told them that I was at a Thai restaurant across the street. When they stopped by is when I realized that there were still walls. His wife explained how I was finally talking and acting how I use to act before I left the church the first time. What I found interesting was that I wasn't doing anything any different than I had been doing before. I believe it was how they viewed me. I began to question and ask God, was the problem me? I was so unsure.

At one Tuesday night Bible Study, my brother called me, and another member up an began to read this scripture that implied that I was not living according to the will of God and that God was going to kill me. I took this to heart because I knew that I was doing everything that I knew how to do to live right. That night I cried all the way home while telling another lady who I had become good friends with what happened. She encouraged me the best way that she could, but I cried like an infant, and when I got home, I just talked to God. What I know now is that my brother used the bible as a way of controlling people. He would tell the members not to listen or visit other churches because he didn't want them to get confused with the teaching. I listened and did everything that my brother said to do, not realizing that I needed only to be listening to the voice of God.

The spirit of God would speak to me often, and the word of knowledge that he would say to the church, and I privately was always, "I AM GOD." I now know that he was telling the people and me to place our hope and trust in him and not in man. Salvation is a gift, and I was taught to believe that if I didn't live right, I would lose my salvation, but God is not an Indian giver, as the older people would say. We often think that God leaves us, but even when we are in the midst of our sin, he is still standing by, like he was for me when I returned.

My time at this church was rocky. There were good times and times when I felt that I shouldn't be there. I wish I could say that the good time outweighed the bad times, but they didn't. One Sunday after church, when Baby Girl was visiting during a church anniversary service, a table was set up for the family to dine together. My brother's wife made it a point to leave Baby Girl and me out, despite others trying to offer us a seat and would do it again one New Year's Eve service. Her response to me was that I wasn't immediate family. Not knowing any better, I always agreed, but I'm sure with the wrong attitude. It wasn't so much of the seating; it was the dismissal and non-inclusion that bothered me.

Others in the church would see these things and seek me out to talk about it, which is how I would fall into the trap. In addition to the seating, she would say in her messages, "It doesn't matter what kind of clothes you wear, what kind of car you drive or education that you have. What matters is in your heart". I completely agreed with her and was asked one day by another member, "Do you realized that she is talking about you?". No, I didn't think she was talking about me because I thought our relationship was okay until the day at the Thai restaurant. We did not feel the same way about each other. Her oldest daughter and I, who I had loved dearly for many years, was having issues. She would leave me in charge of the choir and praise team while she was away with specific instructions, but the members would complain, instead of her asking why, I felt attacked on multiple occasions. There was an email exchanged between my oldest niece and I that was highlighted and taken to the Pastor, my brother. Instead of discussing the concerns with me, I was interrogated and crossed examined by my brother. I had grown to love her and was quite disappointed in the direction of our relationship. I will admit that I could have handled the response; differently. She was someone that I had defended growing up because I felt the constraints placed on her life were unreasonable. When she graduated from college, I also gifted her a car. The red Mitsubishi Mirage that I had worked so hard to pay-off. Her mother had been so helpful to me by co-signing; I felt obligated to do so. One evening while at my house, she asked, "Aunt Tonya, since you did not give me anything for graduation, can I have your car." I guess her mother put her up to this because I had purchased another car; why on earth would I need two cars? Well thinking back, I should have sold the car because that is what she ended up doing later after driving it for a while. I felt like I was on a roller-coaster ride that would never end.

The final straw for me was one Sunday, my niece was out of town, and I was in charge. Apparently, someone reported that we were eating candy while in the choir stand, and I was reprimanded for allowing them to do that. The concern shared here was that every Sunday, my youngest niece would eat in the choir stand, so no one thought anything was wrong with it.

Well, the answer was that my youngest niece was different and needed to eat, so her blood sugar didn't drop too low. The next incident took place on Mother's Day. I placed my cell phone on the chair next to me and was receiving Happy Mother's Day text messages, and while checking my phone, I saw her as she watched out of the corner of her eye, but what was wrong with me looking at my phone. I wasn't sitting there on my phone texting, and I was sitting on the back row. Again, this was a way to control me. Not only was I not allowed to visit or listen to other Pastors, now I couldn't use my phone while in service. Come on; this is church people! Little did I know, God was foreshadowing what was to come. On a good Sunday, the church might have 50 people that attended the service. The church had a revolving door, people would come, and people would go. Behind the scenes, the gossipers would egg me on. I recall the statement, why would your niece ever respect you when her mother doesn't? She would talk about me, and the conversations would find their way to me and vice versa. In my heart, I believed that God had called me back to the church, but for a season. There was a lot that I needed to learn and healing that needed to take place. Seasons change, and I began to understand that my time there was coming to an end.

Every October, my brother's wife or the First Lady would have a Women's Conference, and this would be my second year invited to speak. Before going to the conference, the Women's Ministry had planned a trip to the Woman Thou Art Loose Conference held under Mega Fest this year in Texas. When booking my flight, I mistakenly booked one day later than the rest of the ladies. My hotel was booked correctly, arriving when everyone else was scheduled, so I had to rebook, and called my brother's wife. I could tell she was irritated, but mistakes happen. When I arrived in Texas and made it to the lunch spot, she came out to meet me. It's one thing when you are liked and another when you are just tolerated. No matter what I did to work on our relationship, once again, I was tolerated. To work on our relationship, I asked if she would like to go to lunch one Saturday, and she responded, "Let me think about it." I know, right? Why did I even bother, but I was trying to make things right between us. She finally accepted the offer, and we headed out to an area in Virginia that I recalled her saying that she didn't like driving to because she would always get lost, so I thought that it was a good idea to take the drive. I picked her up in my convertible BMW, which I also knew bothered her. Did she feel a sense of competition with me, I wondered? Before my mother passed away when I attended the first storefront church, I bought my first luxury car, a red Lexus Coupe. Soon after, my brother purchased a Lexus ES for her. When they saw me again years later, I had upgraded to a Lexus RX truck, and after returning to the church, the day before my daughter graduated college, I purchased a convertible BMW.

The day that I drove the BMW to the church, I didn't tell anyone that it belonged to me. My brother walked up to me before the morning prayer and asked if that was my car? When I said yes, he responded, "Can you afford it." He never said congratulations, only can you afford it. Maybe my brother was concerned about my well-being; I'm not sure. I responded, "Have you seen my tithes?" If you are not familiar with Tithes, they are a 10th of every dollar that you receive, and I was a regular tither. God had even asked me to bless him one day, and I wrote him a check for $1000 just because I believe God told me to give it to him. I had always been generous, which could also be the reason why my brother's wife's oldest daughter asked me for my car.

One Christmas, I wanted to have the entire family come together since everyone was so estranged, so I planned a Christmas dinner the night before me, and Baby Girl was heading to Hawaii. After my mother passed, holidays were never the same. When my mother was alive, at Christmas, she would be over at my house, and after my brother visited his wife's family, he would come over as well. Now that my mother is no longer with us, Christmas ended up being Baby Girl, me, and several of her friends. They loved my cooking, and after they opened their gifts and ate with their families, my house was the next stop, filled with young teenagers and bags of Tupperware. My daughter's friends made sure that they left no leftovers behind. After feeding her friends for nearly four years, we decided to go away for Christmas, and we still agree that this was the best thing we could have ever done.

The Christmas party included family that hadn't been in the same room together in nearly ten years and guess who decided to arrive over an hour late. Yes, you guessed right, my brother and his family. Then when they arrived, it was as if they didn't want to mingle with the others. My brother's younger years were shady; he overcame many obstacles and changed his life around. Could it have been that he was ashamed to be around people that knew his past? What I thought would be an amazing party ended up being underwhelming. To respect my brother, I had carefully selected the music and told everyone that there would be no alcohol. I'm not sure why I spent so much of my time trying to please them. Later after talking to a guy that I had just met for the first time for 4 hours. I had the answer! He told me that I stayed because I was seeking validation. I'm sure you knew this as early as chapter 3, but for some reason, it has just become apparent to me. I have stayed in uncomfortable and disapproving relationships because I was looking to be validated. Could it be because my mother never said I love you, or was it because my grandmother stopped allowing me to visit at 13 years old? Maybe it was all the failed relationships that I had been in that both verbally and physically abused me. Needing to be validated is something God delivered me from. The only validation that I need is from Jesus, who is my father, friend, and counselor. If Jesus says he is pleased, then it is well with my soul.

Lunch with my brother's wife was a struggle, the conversation was awkward, but I continued to try to please her. We talked about the company that I had recently started, and I explained how someone with her background could be a consultant one day. She wasn't very entrepreneurial and had worked the same job since high school. I didn't have that type of consistency and being at DOJ was the most extended place that I had worked for more than five years. As a result, I had gotten bored after receiving my MBA and was going stir crazy to do more.

Consequently, I started my own company that help other small businesses increase revenue by gaining contracts with the federal government. I could tell that my brother's wife wasn't interested, and it made me feel like I was bragging, so I ended that topic of discussion. She appreciated me more when I didn't have anything and needed somewhere to stay. Me being successful wasn't something that she could celebrate. After lunch, we walked around the mall. I had my eye on a designer Gucci bag that I was saving up to purchase. When she saw the price of the bag, I saw her mood change. She later asked me how much I paid for the Hawaii trip and talked about how she couldn't get my brother to fly so they could leave the country.

The day seemed long, but it was a beautiful day with sunshine but not warm enough to put the top down. While driving back, my mind was racing as I was thinking about topics of concern to discuss with her, this might be my only chance. Before she got out of the car, I asked her about some of the points in her message. I asked when she made the statement, "No one cares what kind of clothes you wear, the education that you have or the type of car that you drive," what did she mean. She said, "Let me think about it," and exited the car. I drove off with disappointment because I wanted the lunch to help restore our damaged relationship, but it seemed to make us even more distant. Outwardly she seemed supportive, but I could see that I was tolerated.

Mother's Day Sunday after service, my brother's wife's daughter, asked if I could stay after service along with another leader that stayed behind. In the most inappropriate confrontational manner, I was cornered, she confronted me about being on my phone. I had enough and snapped! I completely forgot that I was in church and was getting ready to put my hands on her until the other leader jumped in between the two of us. I was tired of her disrespecting me. I listened to her as the leader but didn't understand the enforcement of all the controls. It seemed as if I was the one targeted, and I believed her mother initiated the controls. I am so glad that the other leader jumped in between us because I would have given her a beaten of her life. She always had a smart mouth but couldn't back it up, and I had planned to show her what it meant to catch a beat down. Besides, unlike my oldest nephew, who would refer to me as auntie, she would only call me by my first name. Initially, this didn't bother me but was brought to my attention by the church gossipers. What I failed to realize was that a dog that brings a bone was also the dog that carried the bone. Every conversation that I would have was taken back and created strife between my family and me.

While in Texas, I realized that not only was there a separation between my brother's wife and me, I also didn't have a real bond with the other women that were there. I was tolerated. Others would say they are just jealous, but I never saw any reason why they would be jealous. I had worked hard for everything that I had from my education, clothes, shoes, and car. I had changed my life and understood that I needed to work for the things that I wanted. I would never take something that didn't belong to me again, including someone else's husband!

Nevertheless, at the conference, there was a new speaker that we had not heard of, hitting the platform, that would change my life forever. Because they didn't know who she was, they were preparing to leave until me, and one other lady decided to stay. The speaker brought back memories from when I was a child watching my mother and great aunt minister the gospel with everything that they had, hands on their hips with leans, and screams they didn't leave anything unturned. During this speaker's sermon, she directed us to place our hand on the belly of the woman next to you and tell her to push. None of the women that I was with were interested in partnering with me. God knew what he was doing and had a woman sitting beside me to do as requested. She began to pray with and for me. I could feel the spirit of God pulling me and delivering me from things that had been shut up in my life, that I was holding on too. God had put his plan into action. For nearly two months, I had been reading in the Old Testament book of Exodus about how God freed the children of Israel. The message title for the Women's conference was, "I am coming out!". I didn't know at the time that while I was preparing the message that God was sending me to another place. What I learned was that when it's time to go, you need to go, or the situation will become so uncomfortable that you will be forced to leave.

The women from the church left a day before me since I had mistakenly booked my flight to depart a day later. After the conference, I decided to attend Sunday Service at the P-Mega church in Texas. I had never participated in a service at a Mega Church before, besides this was the first time we were allowed to visit another church, so this was a massive step for me.

The church was friendly and had a welcome center that greeted me as a guest and escorted me to guest seating. There were about 10,000 people in service, including celebrity figure Tyler Perry and the speaker that I had just heard. I felt like I was out of my confront zone but also felt at home at the same time. As I worshipped and listened to the message for that day, I felt a sense of peace and freedom as I watched the Leader thank all the volunteers.

When I returned to the church, I had a new state of mind. As the church's Women's Conference approached, one of the women in the church who I had established a relationship with an author, told me that she wanted to share something with me. This author had written a non-fiction book that gave a bio of her life story. The book was dynamic and impactful. As a result, she was driven to get her book out to the masses and asked me if I could help her. Because I didn't want to do anything that was out of line, I asked her to get my brother's permission. She explained how when she asked him that his response was no and that I didn't have her best interest at heart. That it would be better if he had his wife help or another lady at the church. The author said that she didn't want to hurt me, so she had held on to it. When she told me, I was trying to stay in a place of prayer and meditation for the upcoming speaking assignment and decided not to say anything. She never said to keep it a secret, but I kept it to myself. God spoke through me at the conference, and the women were blessed. They received the word because the altar was full of women ready to surrender, as tears flowed down their faces. I know that I am only a vessel of God, and nothing happened by my might, but it was by surrendered heart that God was able to use me. Sadly, I noticed at the early part of my sermon the entire front row was disengaged, but I tried not to allow them to distract me. My brother's wife had her clique or mean girls club as the other women called it who weren't part of the group. Nonetheless, I prayed for the women and, as normal, asked my brother's wife to work the altar with me. She, of course, never knew why, and as I understand, tried to have an altar call at a future service where the power of God did not move in the same way.

After the conference, I sent my brother a text message about what the author told me he said about me not having her best interest. I was hurt to hear that he would say something like that about me and thought that I had done the right thing by waiting. Instead of my brother responding, his wife decided to give me a call. You would think that she would have learned her lesson after the last time she did something like this. Instead of being provoked by her, I decided that I would take the high road, not knowing her point in calling. When she called, she seemed upset that I would believe that my brother would ever say such a thing and had warned me about the author. When I first came back to the church, and my brother saw that I was getting close to this author and warned me that she was a trouble maker, he called her crazy and said whenever she comes around, she always gets her mother and sister off track. I didn't know anything about her, and she seemed to be the opposite of how he described her, so I didn't let him stop me from being her friend. Besides, I read her book, and she seemed to have gone through and overcome a lot in her life. Discontented, my brother's wife said that she was going to call her and put an end to this. Somehow the tables were turned when she called. I still don't know what was said when they spoke, but on that Saturday, I noticed that my brother was very distant from me. I tried to talk to him, and although he wasn't mean, I could sense that he was removed. We did street ministry or outreach as they called it on Saturdays with the other ministers in training. Yes, I was still in training after having preached my first message in 2003. I didn't think that there was anything wrong with it because I had left the church for five years. Unlike the prodigal son, I wasn't celebrated for my return; instead, I was still in a position to prove myself or be validated.

The next day was Sunday, and we would generally have dinner or brunch at my brother's after service, but there was something about today that didn't sit well with me. I had cooked a jambalaya in the crockpot and had such an uneasy spirit that I asked my oldest nephew if he could take it to the house. For the first time, he told me that he couldn't do so. That he didn't have room in the van for the crockpot, so I decided to suck it up, not run and go to the house. On my way, in my conversation with God, I committed to staying there until 6 pm. We had brunch, and I could still sense that something wasn't right. After I ate, I went to the living room and laid down on the floor. When it was time for me to go, I heard my youngest niece say out loud, "Aunt Tonya, are you about to leave," I responded and told her yes, I had homework due at midnight. I was in the process of getting a Masters in Theology, which was also something my brother questioned should I do, but I wanted to learn more than what he was teaching. My brother and his wife approached me and asked if they could speak to me downstairs.

In the downstairs basement sat a $4000 sectional that I had donated to his church before returning as well as the dining room table and accent pieces. Unreal! I had requested that the items be donated to someone less fortunate that went to his church, but as it turned out, he gave it all to his youngest daughter to furnish her apartment in college if I wanted to do that I would have given the furniture to my daughter. Over the years, as God blessed me enough to get new furniture, I had committed to helping someone else less fortunate. The first time that I was able to purchase living room furniture after college for my first apartment in Maryland had also been donated to a single mom that lived in the apartment community. I had lived there for 17 years, and the furniture was still in excellent shape. I donated the living room furniture and accent tables. Now I get to sit on the furniture that should have been donated and listen as my brother looks at me with utter disgust. He asked me what I had he ever done to me that would cause me to talk about him the way that I have. I repeatedly asked what I said, and neither he nor his wife would tell me. That day undid everything that I had worked on spiritually for the last four years of my life. I had already been both mentally and physically abused, and now I was spiritually abused. I sat in the basement and cried like a newborn baby. It was so bad that my brother's wife asked my brother to stop, but it was too late. When I left, part of me died. It felt like the light inside of me had been turned off. I cried for the next few days and then put my feelings away as I would usually do not knowing that I had become a trash masher. Never be a trash masher; confront the situation! That week I acted as if everything was okay, but I turned to the one thing that I always looked for in comfort. I went on a dating site and found a guy that was fine as red wine! I hadn't dated or been with anyone since my last break up, four years ago. I thought that I had put all that I had in building my relationship with God only to realize that I was trying to build a relationship with my family.

Thanksgiving and I was headed to my brothers with my regular glazed ham cover with pineapple and cherries. I also had my famous mac&cheese that I included five different kinds of cheese. I was skipping today because later that night, I had a date with Mr. Fine. I had moved on to dating apps now. I met him on Match.com. We had been talking now for two weeks, and I finally agreed to go to the movies with him. After we had finished dinner and played a game, I told my family that I was leaving, that I had a date. I could see the look on my brother's face, but I didn't care at this point. Besides, this was the same man that had ripped my heart out in the basement, the same man that took my donated furniture and gave it to his daughter, the same man that asked me to lie to his wife. So, I left! After the movie, I wasn't sure if I would see him again. It was a large part of me that wanted to remain free. I felt that if I dated someone that it would change the relationship that I had developed with God for the last four years. I didn't want to fall subject or fall back into the woman that I use to be. I wanted nothing to do with her.

The year was closing fast, and now it's New Year's Eve. We had a celebration service at church. Mr. Fine had invited me out that night to a party, and I told him that I would let him know if I was going to attend. Well that night, my brother's wife asked me to move from where the family was seated and sit on the other side so that my youngest niece's boyfriend could sit with the family. Embarrassed, as usual, I moved and sat on the other side. My brother never stood up for me; I was his only living sister as my two other sisters were both deceased, and I was the youngest of five. One would think that he would have supported me more, but he didn't. After service, to make myself feel better, I went to the party. Mr. Fine had graduated from Howard University, had pledged Omega, earned a Master's in Education, and was a real estate developer who owned multiple Airbnb's around the city. We danced the night away, and after, I went back to his place. What I thought was that he would have taken advantage of a broken-hearted woman, but he didn't. We slept, and he held me close. The next morning, he introduced me to a new way of life. He was in the kitchen juicing. Yes, Mr. Fine was also a healthy eater. I guess that's what made him so fine!

After time went on, we began to spend a lot more time together, and in February, I crossed the line and had sex with him. I had fallen again, but I was determined not to continue down this path, so I immediately repented to God that Sunday. I went up to the altar and asked God to forgive me, but deep down, I had condemned myself. My flesh had always been my weakness, and I just felt defeated. I had failed.

On a monthly basis, I had agreed to have lunch with my brother; so that we could work on our relationship and develop a closer bond. Well, at lunch, it was obvious that something was wrong with me. My brother asked me repeatedly, but I would say I'm fine, nothing is wrong. At lunch this month, when he asked me again, I admitted what was wrong. I told him about Mr. Fine and how I had fallen. I also told him that I had repented. That evening he called and said to me that he had to sit me down from MIT. I agreed, I never wanted to do anything that was opposite of what he believed to be what God wanted me to do.

The following Sunday, I was also told that I could not join the circle in prayer. Not only did I need to be sat down from being a minister, now I was not even allowed to pray. Isn't God a forgiving God?! That day after Sunday service, he called and told me that God said he needed to sit me down from being part of the Worship Team but that I could remain in the choir. Then it all began to unravel. He told me that God said that I had sex in November. I asked him three times to be sure that he was certain that God told him that. The God that I serve cannot lie, so I knew that God hadn't told him that.

For once, I stood up for myself and told him that was not true. I then said to him that if I wasn't good enough to be on the Worship team, then I would sit myself down from everything else. That I would no longer be in the choir, the assistant to event planning, nor would I be his secretary. As the week went by, I found it strange that I hadn't heard from his wife. I knew she was behind him sitting me down from the Worship Team because I didn't show enough remorse that Sunday at church. I recall her not even being able to give me eye contact. We spoke that week, and she began to tell me how dare I tell her husband that he doesn't hear from God. She went on to say that I never live right, and it was always because of a man. She also finally responded to my question about who was she referring to in her messages when she would say, "It doesn't matter what kind of clothes you wear, what kind of car you drive, what kind of education you have," to say, "It's not like you live in a house on a hill or that you are dripping with diamonds." I stopped her and asked where was all this coming from? At this point, I wasn't even angry but determined to get my life back on track. Matthew 12:34 (ASV) states, How can you speak good things when you are evil? For out of the abundance of the heart, the mouth speaks. She said what she meant. This woman had been jealous of me all along. Before she hung up as I explained that I wasn't going to leave the church, she told me that she hoped that I didn't come back, so I didn't. I initially had no intention of leaving and just needed some time to digest what had happened.

When I think about how they treated me, I am reminded of the woman that was brought before Jesus and accused of committing adultery in John 8:1-11. They made this woman stand before them, the Scribes and Pharisees, while telling Jesus that she had been caught in the very act. The law of Moses during this time commanded that they stone the woman. As they spoke, Jesus never gave them eye contact, stooped down, and began to draw on the ground with his finger. When he responded, he asked if there was one who had never sinned and, if so, to throw the first stone, then went back to writing on the ground. As the accusers heard this, they began to depart one by one. I believe that Jesus was writing their name in the dirt for those that had sinned. Besides, how did they catch her in the act anyway? Which one of them was there with her at the time? When Jesus stood up, he asked the woman, where are your accusers, didn't one of them stay to condemn you? The woman responded no, and Jesus said neither do I, now go and sin no more.

As I am reminded of this scripture, if Jesus has forgiven me and is not condemning me, why am I allowing a man or woman to condemn me? So, from that point on, I decided that it was no turning back. One week later, I sent an email and advised that I was removing my membership. Instead of my brother allowing me to leave peacefully, the Sunday after he told the entire MIT team that he had sat me down from everything, to leave me alone and not talk to me. Why would I return to a church where when people depart, the Pastor tells them not to speak to that person anymore. I wasn't the first person that he did this too, I just never thought he would do it to me. According to Webster, a cult is defined as a system of religious veneration and devotion directed toward a particular figure or object. A relatively small group of people having religious beliefs or practices regarded by others as strange or sinister. Now, reading that definition, I am not saying it's a cult, but when you tell your members that they can't listen to other Pastors, visit other churches, and then not to talk to the people when they leave, you decide.

Little did he know a few of us had snuck out and went to York Pennsylvania to see the speaker that was at Mega Fest. I found out that she was a Pastor of a church that was less than two hours away. We promised not to tell anyone, and I went back multiple times, not knowing what was to come with the spiritual abuse that would result in my departure. One night at Manna on Monday, I went up to the altar for prayer, and at the end, the guest speaker said to turn to the person next to you and give them a hug. There wasn't anyone next to me other than the speaker that I had heard at WTOL. She didn't hug me; she shook my hand. When I walked away, my spirit said that is part of your assignment, but I didn't know what it all meant then.

After I decided not to go back to my brother's church, I would get phone calls despite his instructions as the members would tell me how he would preach about me across the pulpit. On one occasion, he even told them that they must be careful not to let witches come into the church and leave with the members. Apparently, now I was a witch. The crazy part about this is that I didn't take any members.

The people that left were already on their way out the door. What he did by preaching about me was to push them out the door by showing a lack of love. One member that I was close too had gone to him on multiple occasions for counseling and help. He had disregarded her once and made her feel low as scum. After that day, I would go to her house before service to encourage her to attend. No one knew that I was doing this. During this time, I hadn't given up hope in the church and wanted to make sure that she attended. When I left, I wasn't there to do that anymore, and as a result, she stopped going. They blamed me for her leaving, and apparently, I was responsible according to my brother's wife for 50% of the church leaving. Who has that type of power? Did they once think that maybe the people left because of them? There was only one person that left soon after me, but even with her, she had one foot out the door anyway.

I wasn't in touch with the members of the church after I left. I wanted to separate myself and heal. One month earlier, I received a notification from the couple that had rented my home in Virginia that they were planning to move out. I was potentially facing a situation where I had two properties that I would have to pay for. Therefore, I tried to rent the property but was unable to do so. My realtor explained that although the property wasn't renting that properties in the community were selling. If I had only known that my relationship with my family was about to fall apart, I would have kept the property. Since I had no idea and was not able to pay rent and a mortgage, I decided to sell my first home. Why did I ever leave my home, to begin with, it was a bad life decision. I once believed that I did the right thing by going to help my brother. Now, after five years, I've realized that our emotions can drive our hearts. One month later, the reason for my move was falling apart.

My rent at the place in Maryland was also coming to an end. Here I am, February 2014, just sold my home and leaving the church. All of this happened in one month. What was God up too?

Chapter 21

Finding My Way

Now it was time for me to live unchained and free. My departure was like my arrival; I received no assistance and had to pack alone. I had some time on my hand between the move-out and move-in. Baby Girl ensured that I had a fresh start. I gave her my American Express, and she designed and decorated my new home. When I left, I didn't share my location with anyone because I wanted to be free! During her design plan, I learned that my home never truly represented who I am as a person. Finally, at 42 years old, I learned that my favorite color was blue. I was excited that for once in my life, I was discovering who I am. I'm telling you today that you need to Know Who You Are! My home would now represent my life loves, with shades of blue, gold accents with a modern flair, and a traditional stance. My surroundings now represent me as a bold, strong, beautiful woman that wants to live her life to the fullest, and through it all, I made myself a promise that this time I would not leave the church.

While looking at one of my social media accounts, I realized that the speaker from WTOL was going to be preaching at Jericho, one of the largest churches in the DC metro area, on Easter Sunday. After seeing that, I immediately knew where I was going on Easter. Arriving at this church on Easter Sunday brought back the mega church memories that I once had when I visited the P-mega church in Texas. The service was incredible, and I continued to attend month after month. What I didn't know until Easter Sunday was that the conference speaker was selected as the interim Leader. The church was going through a legal fight of ownership, where the founder was deceased, and the son wanted to be the Leader. I had never heard of a church board who could vote a Leader in or out. My brother had no such thing; he wasn't even accountable to anyone besides himself. I didn't want to know any more about what was happening with the church legally. Unlike everyone else, I wasn't reading the online blogs or watching the videos that were full of scandals. I was focused and wanted no parts of the gossip. Mr. Fine had even reached out a few times, but after finding out that he was a liar and an atheist, I felt like a complete fool and moved on. He had an entire family in Belize that I knew nothing about.

On Sunday, there was an announcement, requesting volunteers for an upcoming book release, and I decided to go. When I arrived, I sat alone but was willing to start serving as a volunteer in the church. It was there that I forged some friendships. The book release was for one of the most significant Leaders and was going to be an important event. As we gathered, I met a friend that I would grow to call Sista for years to come. What I found to be crazy was, instead of me being reprimanded for looking at my phone in church, I was being asked by the conference speaker, now interim Leader's assistant to be part of her social media team. I didn't know much about social media other than I had been using twitter to tweet out the sermon points. Clearly, my Sista's and my tweets had been recognized, and before we knew it, we were on the road helping with product sales and updating her social media page.

The book release was crowded, but I was able to see what happens behind the scene at an official book launch. I didn't know that I would be using everything that I would learn over the next four years for the rest of my life. Often in life, we go through things and ask God why when it is all part of his plan. The process over the next four years compelled me to release and write this book. While finding myself, it became evident that my gifts had been buried by all my insecurities, and it was my fault, but I thank God for my gravedigger that would unbury me.

Feeling like a fish out of water on the newly formed social media team, I was still grateful to support but knew that I had so much more to offer. I was now serving in multiple capacities and was in an unfamiliar place. I believe that this was ordained by God to place me here for a season. As I listened to this Woman of God, I realized that I had been taught a lot of bad theology in my life. I wanted to be part of a ministry that I felt was more suitable for me, so I attended choir rehearsal. The choir was being newly formed after the church split from the legal battles. The strangest thing happened while I was in rehearsal; it was as if I could no longer sing. I had no voice. I recall the last time I lead a song at my brother's church; I could barely get the words out because I was weeping on the inside. The title of the song was, I Need More of You. I needed to know that God was with me more than ever. I was trying to hold on to everything that I knew about him that was good, not the training that led me to believe that God lacked love. As I write today, I can say that God is restoring my voice. It is one thing to sing and it is another to have a gift. I don't feel like my voice is what it used to be, but I enjoy worshiping God more now than ever before. I believe that God will fully restore my voice one day. Besides, for five years, I had sung in bad microphones that caused a strain on my vocal cords.

After one practice with the newly formed choir, I decided to focus on social media. I was being buried deeper but didn't even know that it was happening. Later, I learned that the Women's ministry met every other Saturday, and I decided to attend. During the service, the Woman of God announced that they were recruiting more women for the ministry. Months had gone by before this happened, and I had already traveled to Atlanta to support her ministry product sales and social media updates. When I sent my email of interest, I made sure to give her my name and tell her that I was the one that helped with her product table because I didn't believe that she even knew my name. I wasn't there for her popularity like most people who loved her ministry. I was there because I wanted to serve. I was desperately trying to prove something to God. Who was I to think that I could prove anything to God, isn't he all-knowing?

Finally, when I walked into my new, beautifully decorated home, I arrived after having surgery. I had to have a partial hysterectomy. That resulted from fibroids and the years of aggressive sex that had caused a massive amount of scar tissue. My past was now catching up to me. My periods were so bad that I had to stay home the first three days, and even after that was a risk of messing up my clothes. The pain was as if I was giving birth to a child every month. One day before I moved, I almost passed out, but thankfully I was right next door to Urgent Care. When I walked in, the front desk person yelled for help, and they immediately put me in a wheelchair and rolled me in the back. I must have dozed off or fainted, I'm not sure, but when I woke up, they had placed an IV in my arm. The doctor was asking me if I was pregnant, and I repeatedly told him no. I knew that wasn't the issue, but he wasn't convinced until they had me take a pregnancy test. Then it was determined that I was dehydrated from the blood loss. I had also become extremely anemic. I realized more than ever that moving was right for me at that moment when I had no one to call. Baby Girl lived closer to the city, and I was at least 40 minutes away.

My first two days home from surgery were spent in the bed on pain meds and Baby Girl making sure that I had what I needed. After two days of recovery, I was back to myself, able to walk around and look at how lovely everything was and how God had blessed me. It was a fresh start, my new place gave me peace and rest, but it still did not feel the void and emptiness that I had. One would think that now since I had found a new church and met new friends that I could mature and leave the nonsense in the past, but it didn't happen exactly this way. I started to look at dating apps more and more. It felt like a way for me to screen the guys that I would date. I tried Match.com; I even tried SugarBaby. com and lied about my age. Not only could I screen the guys, but it was also like shopping. I could select them by height, appearance, social status, job, and even wealth. I found this to be fun and exciting all at the same time. Three men stood out. Two were business owners, and one was a doctor. You will read more about this later.

I felt like a new woman. The stress that I had been under in a place where I never wanted to live had suddenly lifted off me. Now I was able to serve freely in the ministry and was not being judged. My Sista friend and I were asked to sit at the top of the stairs in the back of the sanctuary in the glass media room during service to support the ministry requirements. Being there made me feel cut-off from the service and the message. Although we sang to our hearts' delight in the glass room, it wasn't the same.

Being at a megachurch gave me access to what happened behind the scenes allowing me to see things that I wasn't necessarily ready for. I was just stoned after falling to my flesh even after having repented to God, to now finding myself in a place where it seems like anything goes. The board began to put restrictions on the Woman of God complaining that the new membership mainly consisted of homosexuals. The scandals and media would say that the Woman of God was a lesbian, but what I knew is that I was supposed to be there. I would always say that when God tells me to leave, I will leave and never look back. I decided to ignore the gossip, rumors, and things that were in plain sight. The story was that the current assistant had once been the assistant and girlfriend of another Mega Evangelist that made the now famous women's conference what it had become today with her historic message. Listen, I had decided to mind my own business and not to read anything on the internet. When I was at my brother's church, there was a young woman that was there briefly trying to bring the church up to a higher standard with its administration and media. We talked about her discontentment with the church, and she shared with me that the mothers of the church were often predators of the younger women, and I was astounded. I could not imagine anything of the sort. Seeing it firsthand, I now understood what she meant. I wasn't directly approached but could see it all around me.

I referred to the church as the Big Blue Dinosaur. I could tell that once upon a time, it was something to talk about with the glass walls in the hallways and gold trimmings, but in its current state, it could use some paint and a thorough carpet cleaning. As I continued to attend the Women's Ministry events, the leader began to see the call of God on my life. God had to reveal what was behind the smile that I struggled to wear every time I walked in the door because I never told anyone that I was a minister, but one day she asked me to pray. Pray? I was thinking that's simple enough and won't create any drama for me. I wanted to stay away from anything that would draw me into a gossip mill or get me entangled with the wrong people. So, on this Saturday, I prayed with everything that I had in me and things changed after that. The women in this ministry were older and seasoned, which was great. I was able to sit back and watch them work with love, something that I had not seen in action at my former church. It always seemed like everyone was competing against each other or the mean girls club. I believe that the day I prayed, when I opened my mouth, they knew that I had been called by God. From that day on the leader would take me under her wing and mentor me. I'm not sure if she ever quite knew how shattered and broken, I was. Deep down, I believe that this ministry leader knew and that I was her assignment. I lacked confidence and had so many insecurities. What I know now that I didn't realize then is that I had placed my trust in man and not on God. Over the next few years, I would have so much to unload and learn.

When they learned that I could pray, I asked to pray at the Sunday service. Me praying as the new kid on the block was a challenge, it often felt like them against us. There was no togetherness after the founder died. The son left with over half of the congregation, and only a few of the original members remained. Even now with the Woman of God, they had to start over with about 50-100 members, if that. The divide was evident to everyone. Them against us was as if they did not believe that we were even saved nor lived a holy enough life to pray, serve, or do anything in the church. While I was praying that Sunday, I could see the eyes rolling and the discontentment. My heart went out to the Woman of God because they worked hard to control everything that she did, even her sermons. Still trying to find my way, I spent most of my time connecting with the young adults' ministry, although I was far from the young adult status. Now my insecurity needed acceptance, and I felt caught in-between as the age groups were either 20 years older than me or younger than me.

I was excited when I found out that the Women's Ministry meeting to add new ministry leaders was happening, so I decided to show up. I was so desperate that I didn't know where the meeting was being held and only the time, so I follow the crowd of ladies. I did not know that the current members were asked to invite a potential member. I was there without anyone inviting me. After the Woman of God made the announcement for those that were interested in the ministry, I did not hesitate. I emailed her and figured that was enough. When we arrived in the conference room, everyone was going around the table announcing themselves, and the Woman of God knew that no one had invited me. I believe that she made them go around in the circle for that very reason. One thing that I learned about her over the years was she was quite the hazer.

A current member looked at me while everyone was going around to announce themselves and mouthed, I invited you. I was relieved, and I whispered back okay, but when it was her turn, the Woman of

God replied, "And you didn't bring anyone because I brought you." There I was, I could have disappeared into the seat—another notch on the list of my insecurities. I began to wonder what God was doing in my life or was this all self-inflicted pain. The only thing I knew was that I was trying to hold on and do what I believed was the right thing. What was the right thing, this is what I mean by bad theology? God is love, bottom line! When it was my turn, I boldly announced that no one brought me and that I had sent an email. I then went on to say, "I am saved, filled with the Holy Ghost with the evidence of speaking in tongues." Really, why did that matter, they looked at me like I had two heads. In my heart, I started to say, and I guess I don't belong here either. When it was over, and we were on our way out, I met another Sista who was bold and confident in her ways. The next meeting was only for a select few, and I was not invited. I felt the same rejection that I had felt in college when I was not selected into the sorority. Was it okay for me to feel this way in church? People its Church! I thought the church was there to build a person up and not tear them down.

The consistency and loyalty that I desired began to shrink more and more. One of my friends encouraged me to go out on the town with her. I hadn't hung out in some time now. We ended up at a restaurant, and there were no more seats left at the bar. While standing there, this guy waved and asked if I needed a chair and motioned us over. He had part of the bar sectioned off while he and his team enjoyed happy hour. He invited us over and began to buy us drinks. My friend seemed disinterested in the free cocktails and moved to our table that was now ready. I didn't want to be rude to her and explained that I was going to go to the table. He soon had the waiter come over and tell us anything that we ordered was on him. Talk about a gentleman! Before we left after he paid the bill, he asked me for my phone number. For the next week, we texted, and he invited me out to a Nationals Baseball Game. This date needed to be perfect; sadly, I hadn't met anyone that had ever shown this type of interest in me. It rained the day of the game, and

I decided that I didn't want to go. I had no idea that our seat was in a covered area. I was thinking that I would be outside sitting on wet bleachers with an umbrella. I could tell that he was disappointed, but instead of going to the game, we ended going to the Gaylord at the National Harbor to watch the game at the sports bar. Before we left the bar, he slid me his drivers' license and said, "I guess this will be our last date." Wow, when I looked at his license, he was about 15 years younger than me. That's not a big deal, right? So, I allowed him to take me out again, and again until we became hanging partners.

We were getting close to the Women's Conference, and I was called back in as part of the team to do social media. What I had not realized was that my Sista friend was upset that I was asked to do the social media and not her. It wasn't my doing, and it wasn't something that I even cared to do. I tried to act as if nothing was wrong until one day without telling me; I was re-assigned from doing social media and placed as the front reception desk as a greeter. That day at the meeting, the Woman of God called in my Sista friend to take over the social media. I wasn't upset, but what I saw that day was a side of her that I would not see again until four years later. I will never forget the look of betrayal that I saw on her face that day. I couldn't understand it then, but I know it now. I thought I was a good friend to her. I was always looking out for her. She often needed a ride, and I would pick her up for church and drop her off back at home even when I would pull up to the house with 2-3 cars in the yard. Unfortunately, her husband wouldn't give her a ride nor anyone else at home. I even looked out for her when we went on the first trip to Atlanta for product sales. We had to purchase our airline tickets, and they would pay us back after the trip.

I purchased the tickets for both of us, so that she could go as well and waited for the Woman of God to give me my almost $700 back. After I saw her face and the fact that she would betray me, I honestly thought that maybe my thinking was wrong. For sure, she was a friend, right? I had been there for her when she was facing a criminal charge due to unpaid car insurance and fines. I paid the fees and penalties for her that nearly totaled $1000. My only ask from her was if I needed some administrative support for workshops that she would assist me. I later realized that this would never happen, and in a service one evening, the Spirit of God told me to gift it to her, so I did.

At the Women's Conference, instead of working at the front desk, I was asked to be the armor bearer for the Woman of God's new assistant. The initial assistant had gotten angry about a potential new relationship that she was not aware of. She felt that the Woman of God was not faithful. When it became a reality, according to my Sista friend, the former assistant was ready to reveal private pictures of the two of them together that would ruin her reputation. My Sista friend disappeared for a day, and when she surfaced, she was in New York with the first assistant and told me about the pictures that she had seen with one of them being dressed like a boy and kissing the other. I was shocked, but that was not my cup to drink from, regardless, I knew that there was a reason for me being there. I was happily out of town the next Sunday. It was rumored that the initial assistant was threatening to go public before her installation. It seemed apparent to me at the installation that the famous Leader was fully aware of what was going on as he spoke over her and implied that sheep sometimes poke their noses in places where they shouldn't and how he was anointing her so that would not happen again. The web became even more entangled; people from her former church were saying that she was in a relationship with her armorbearer. The first assistant learned about this and one other woman, while on a ministry trip with the Woman of God to Canada. Clearly, she was afraid of being exposed. On Sunday, the Woman of God was laid out on the pulpit in a knot crying. The women in the church rushed to her aid and surrounded her to pray, not knowing why she was in that state. What had I gotten myself into?

Assigned to be an armor bearer only exposed me to even more. On the night of the conference, during the social hour, the Woman of God asked me, where was the assistant. When I went to get the assistant, she responded and said, "Every time she says jump, don't mean I jump." So, I said okay and went my way. I didn't want to get caught up in any more church drama, so I kept my mouth closed. That night there was also a visiting First Lady from Europe that gifted the Woman of God with a large sum of money that she would never receive.

The next trip for product sales, I would travel without my Sista friend to Atlanta, and we stayed in a five-star hotel. That trip, I saw another side of the Woman of God and how she operated under her personal ministry. What I learned from the trip is that preaching for some is all about performance and stage presence. The crowd participation on the trip was not what the Woman of God expected the first night, so the second night an additional face towel was brought because she planned to throw it into the crowd in efforts to entertain them. At that moment, I knew that what I saw not just on the road but on a regular Sunday wasn't all spiritual. It was for hype and pretense. This was a real eye-opener for me coming from the church background that I had experienced. After seeing everything that I had seen thus far, I quickly learned to eat the meat and leave the bones. People that knew me would call and ask how I could attend that church and sit under her as a Woman of God. It was simple deep down I believed that I had been called to her even if it was for a season. The one good thing about this trip was that I was supposed to have had a roommate, but my roommate, the Manager, never made it to the room. I'm still not sure why she felt the need to explain, but the Manager indicated that she had fallen asleep in the Woman of God's room. Honestly, I acted as if I didn't hear her, and besides, I had a room at a five-star hotel to myself, so my response was, "Okay!" I didn't want to share a room with her anyway.

I also realized on this trip that I never wanted to do product sales again and when it was time to go, I left without even saying goodbye.

I felt like nothing went right. The credit card machines wouldn't work correctly, the table set up wasn't good enough, and I felt like an utter idiot. I should have been able to lead the product sales with my eyes closed because, in my past, I was responsible for large and small retail store operations. I was very familiar with credit card machines and counting cash, but I couldn't seem to get any of it right on this trip. The night before I left, I counted down the money and gave it to the Manager. My heart was screaming, thank you and farewell!

A few months later, my phone was blowing up, did you hear that the son got the church back? The son had won the case and put padlocks on the church doors after firing everyone that worked there, including the Woman of God. Some of us knew that this would happen and never had faith like the original members that they would keep the church. The church scandal ran deep about the current board being fake, the people staying issuing themselves significant raises, basically being cheaters and thieves. The scandal was all over social media, in the news and papers. The son felt that he had the right to the church that his parents had founded. The board, on the other hand, had determined differently based on what they believed was his mother's dying words. This day was like a circus, and fortunately, the Woman of God had already been notified. When she found out she had her son pack up her belonging before the doors were locked. Fired, that had to be rough after leaving a church that you had pastored for more than ten years and now fired! You think that you know how this possibly feels until something of similar significant loss happens to you. Now what do we do, what do I do, is what everyone was thinking. Were we selfish? Was anyone thinking about what will the Woman of God do? Personally, I was desperately not trying to be without a church. We asked to attend another local megachurch while the Woman of God took time to pray about what to do next. So those that had joined the church under her waited and waited.

That next September, it was announced that there would be an interest meeting. I showed up with the rest of those that had joined the Big Blue Dinosaur while she was there. About 100 – 200 of us showed up, just the right size for a church start-up. She had decided that she would start a church, but she wouldn't call it a church, it was called a CTR.

You could hear the excitement and yells as she entered the room the new theme song, "My name is V." Was this a church meeting or a show? I had been part of the entertainment industry for nearly ten years, and that was my past; tonight, brought back memories which were part of my history that I wanted to move away from. Could this CTR give me what I needed to continue my walk and grow in the direction that God had planned for me? It seemed that everything about ministry for me was on hold, and everything around me seemed to be all for show.

When the doors of the new CTR were opened in a local high school, at the CTR, I served in different capacities but knew that she never saw me. It's rough when you are looking for acceptance and validation from a person that had a lot of healing to do on their own. I waited, and I served. I trusted that I would be okay here. In my quiet time with God, I would hear God say that I have called you to be a light in a dark place. Now, I started to understand what this meant. There were very few that attended the CTR that wanted all of God. When I say all of God, I mean that did not give in to their fleshly desires that were striving to live right. The theme of the church was Grace. I genuinely believe that Grace covers us, but I also know that we are required to do the work. Even Paul asked the question in Romans 6:2 (ASV) Shall we continue in sin, that grace may abound? God forbid. It was as if this scripture did not exist. At times I felt like I was in Sodom and Gomorrah because there was no conviction; it was as if anything goes.

The years seemed to go by while being here at the CTR. On Sunday, the Woman of God would come down from the stage area and greet those that sat on the front row and like clockwork, when she would greet every person, one by one but when she got to my church brother and me, for years she would skip the two of us and then shake the hands of those on the other side of him. I would look and see so much disappointment in his face and tell him it's okay. Deep down, I couldn't quite understand it myself, but her not speaking to me or not knowing my name had become a norm. When I thought that she didn't know my name, she surprised me the day that I was invited back to help with the social media for the conference. She spoke to me when I walked in the door, and I was surprised because I didn't think that she knew my name. The CTR was filled to compacity on Sundays, and the energy in the services was high. I would say the presence of God was high, but what I know now much of what happened was planned. The sermons were always enjoyable as she was the best preacher, teacher that I knew. Yes, she was entertaining, but her messages made you think deeply about the scripture, and the next Sunday, I couldn't wait to get back. She had placed me over the Women's Ministry, and I was able to give the ministry a name. After picking the team, I felt that finally, I would be able to do more to reach the people even if it is all women. I believe that my life lessons and tribulations are there as a testimony to help other women that are hurting and need healing.

Every month we would plan ministry events and would have a relatively large gathering. The very first event was where we put most of our effort to excite the women, or I should say entertain the women. We had the Woman of God come out to theme music, and her Manager was right by her side. We had games, food, guest singers, and pom poms for the women to waive in the air for excitement. We even gave away prizes to the winners of the games. I recall having over 200 women at this event. When I was at my brother's church, his wife, like most First Ladies, was responsible for the women's ministry. I tried to help with a tea event that they had and worked to upgrade it from plastic dollar store table cloths that she wanted and purchased out of my pocket table cloths, chair covers, and decorative items that would make it more similar to a real tea. I thought that I was helpful, but in the last conversation that I had with her, I learned that she felt that I was contradictory. The example that she used was if she said yellow, I would say it should be blue. I never had any intentions of making her feel this way. Those past feelings from the disappointment at my former church, were still alive and active in me while I was at the CTR. My insecurities held me back from doing a lot of things. I should have spoken up more than I did. Having been condemned for being so vocal with my ideas, the boldness that I once exhibited, now was minuscule, I had taken the back seat. I didn't want to step on any one's toes.

We had event after event, and one day the Woman of God called to tell me that she wasn't going to make it, and I had to speak at this event. I immediately started having anxiety. My brother had trained me to think that you should never be excited to preach God's word and to be cautious of the people that were happy to do so. If only I knew then what I know now that it is an honor to be chosen by God to go and preach the gospel and draw people to Christ. The event was full of women, and I even had some women show up that knew me from my brother's church that were no longer members there. The power of God moved at this ministry event. The women were holding on to each other, weeping and crying as God worked on their hearts. They had received the word that God spoke through me on that day. Praise God! For the next event we were asked to set up for a talk show, which was disappointing because we had already planned the entire ministry event. I wasn't surprised because the Woman of God would often change plans at the last minute no matter what it was. The ministry leaders were concerned and quite upset at times. We would work, have multiple planning meetings well in advance and get to the day of the events, and all the plans would be thrown out the window.

Most of the time, the Woman of God was very comical, dancing around and joking with everyone. She would say that if she had not been a preacher that she would have either been a comedian or a pole dancer. I agree the Woman of God would have been good at either. The problem that we faced is that we never knew from day to day if she would be loving or turn around and reprimand you for something. I felt that we spent a lot of time trying to please her when our focus should have been on the people.

I'm very thankful for the years here at the CTR, I learned so much about the operation and administration of ministry both good and bad. My Sista friend and I were thick as thieves, and I had developed friendships with other Sista's as well. Sundays ended up being brunch Sundays. At times, the Woman of God would invite leaders over to her house, and I was the only one that had never been invited. I'm not sure if it was an oversight or if there was a reason behind it, so I never said anything. Clearly, the fact that I am bringing it up now only lets me know that it was another buried insecurity.

During the spring, the Woman of God started preaching a series about faith, and this sermon resonated with me as never before. I was very unhappy at my current job and always felt like I should be doing more. I was a Federal Employee now for over 13 years. My work became a disappointment due to the politics surrounding how Civil Rights cases such as Ferguson and Baltimore were handled. I was responsible for the litigation of these cases, and when speaking with attorneys, I realized that most of them had joined the Civil Rights Division, where I worked only to have it listed on their resume. They were not interested in inner-city cases where innocent black boys were shot. Was I taking this personally because I had two younger nephews that this could happen too? One day, while assigning a case, I received this response, "Why do I need to go to Baltimore when people are dying in Albuquerque NM?" I had watched as they walked around and had conversations about how they, meaning black people, brought all of this on themselves. In my Division, we were responsible for the oversight of police departments, nursing homes, and jails to include juvenile facilities. With all the issues happening in police departments that were already under investigation, it didn't seem like we were doing our jobs very well. I also was facing some internal discrimination where they were promoting a young white guy to be my equal that had less experience and less education. In a meeting one day, while speaking to another manager, she shared how her husband was a Big White Man, and that she tells him every day just how privileged he was. It had gotten to the point where I was depressed and suffering in silence. I had complained so much that even Baby Girl was like, mommy, I can't take it anymore.

I was suffering in silence coming home every day and laying on the floor to cry. During the day, I wore a mask, smiling while in front of others. I was not going to cry nor show my vulnerability. At home, I would cry for hours at a time, and when I wasn't crying, I was complaining to anyone that would listen. Then on Sunday, I would go to church and serve as if nothing was going on. One day I just asked myself was it even worth it. I felt like for most of my life, I had to fight and work and fight, and I was tired. I called my insurance company and asked if I was to commit suicide, would they pay the policy out, and the response was, "no ma'am." The person on the other end of the phone should have called 911, but she didn't. I was depressed that I was not thinking clearly. As it related to the church, I started going through the motions. My personal life had spanned to me, having met three men on a dating app. I dated them from week to week, receiving gifts from them from sizable checks to other material items. I had lost my way, yet again! One of the men was a doctor, and every time he would see me, he would write me a check for $2500 just to be in my company. We would go out for sushi and then back to his house. He worked so much that all he wanted was time with me. He was a tall Italian that stood about 6'9 with a bright smile and was fairly attractive. For me, I was just looking for ways to escape how I felt, 99% of the time, and he was the answer. The other guy was a lot older than me, and we ended up being good friends. He was looking for someone to go to happy hour with him and sometimes dinner. The last guy was a different story; he expected it all and was another married man.

What was I doing? Here I am again after promising myself that I would never date another married man. He was very generous to me, taking me on trips, giving me gifts weekly, spending money on me, and we went out almost every other day. It was easy to date all three because Big Guy, the doctor, had a very tight schedule, and the older guy just wanted to see me from time to time at happy hour. The guy that wanted all my time wasn't my type at all. He was a little overweight and had knocked knees. I wouldn't usually date someone that I wasn't attracted too, but he took my mind off things. Hanging out with him, I was drinking at least 3–4 times a week, not including my newfound love for French Martinis that I was drinking at home. At my doctors' appointment, when they asked how many drinks you have per day and week is when I realized that I was making an alcoholic out of myself. I even noticed that I had developed a slight trimmer in my hands. So, I stopped seeing him so frequently. He wasn't happy about it and assumed that I was seeing someone else when, in fact, I was trying to find me.

Still listening to the sermon series about Faith, one day, I reached out to one of the members at the CTR and was telling him that I was looking for other opportunities and had my own company. He told me he had a company that he wanted to send my resume too. When I did, the owner immediately wanted to talk with me. The company was out of Miami, Florida. For months I had been trying to find my way of escape by connecting with companies that I believed could use my services. The owner of the company, after our initial conversation, planned a meeting in Miami for me to speak with him.

Miami was familiar to me not for business, but where I often went to hang out with friends from New York that I would meet there. When in town, we would have a driver, a security guard, and it was nothing to spend $100K or more in a weekend. Whenever I wanted to let my hair down, it would be with the New York crew. Vegas was another one of our party locations, although we frequented Miami more often. One night got the best of me, and I decided that my party days were over. We started as soon as the plane landed having VIP services during a music festival weekend. I was drinking champagne and doing shots of Don Julio's 1842 Tequila at the first stop from 4:00 pm to 6:00 pm. After we left and dressed for the club, at the next stop, we had two VIP sections and drank shot after shot of tequila with more champagne. When it was time to go, and I stood up, I had no idea that I had drunk so much! I couldn't walk; the security guard had to escort me to the car. As soon as we got to the car, I began to puke the pizza that I had before we left. I was so intoxicated that they had the driver take me back to the hotel. I didn't have my purse, but they let me in the room. That was a terrible night, and I lost control of my bodily functions. They say when that happens, you have alcohol poisoning. The next day when I looked around, I couldn't believe the mess that I had made, and I was so sick. The guys, of course, thought it was funny and began to give me dap saying, "T, that is how you party!" I was so embarrassed that I never accepted another invite.

Chapter 22

The Tables Turn

Not sure what to do next, I found myself on a flight to Miami, Florida. I planned to take Uber or a cab at the airport, but he insisted on picking me up. When I arrived, a white Lexus with dark tinted windows slowly pulled up and out of the car stepped a 6'3 black man in his late 60's with a full beard, very well dressed in a vest and braces or suspenders. He was dark-skinned a Billy Dee Williams type, with his hair combed back. What I found strange was that this man strongly favored the man that I grew up thinking was my father. He asked if I was hungry and we went to lunch.

Wow! I never told you what happened to the man that I thought was my father. Well, his life of women, cocaine, and alcohol had gotten the best of him. He lost everything. I saw him once after he dropped me off for college. The story that I was told is that he had gotten addicted to pain medication. The hospitals across Washington DC, Maryland, and Virginia were turning him away. He was using the hospitals to get prescription opioid's, and eventually, he turned to street drugs. One night, early in the morning, years before he passed, he called asking for $5. Remember, this was the same man that told me that I had to buy $400 shoes that I hated and never wore. His life, as I knew, had fallen apart.

As I understand it, he was basically homeless, living from woman to woman and, at times sleeping in his car. On my 40th birthday, I received a call from one of his sisters, and I was so happy. After all these years, they finally found me! I had been searching for them on social media platforms with no luck, and I get a call on my birthday. Remember, this was a time in my life when I had structure, direction, and felt secure. Unfortunately for me they weren't calling to wish me a happy birthday but to tell me that the man that I thought was my father had been murdered. Someone had broken into his house and shot him in the chest at close range. He was dead. I guess I should have felt sad or shed a tear, but there was nothing. It wasn't that they wanted to let me know that he had passed; they were more interested in his burial insurance. He had lied and told them that everything that he had was in my name. I had not seen nor heard from this man in over ten years. Not only had I not seen him, but I also had no idea where he was. The murder took place in Durham, NC, the town where I had graduated college. He had left his wife and was in a house with a young woman half his age. In good faith, I did check to see if he had insurance by calling the Department of Navy and the Pentagon only to find out that he had cashed out everything that he had. Two weeks before the murder, he had not only cashed out his insurance policies; he emptied his bank account at the Pentagon credit union. The representative didn't know how to tell me the next part; I had a brother. A brother that he had by one of the many women he had married. This brother was in foster care in Durham.

I understood now why he was there, but he was not fit to be a father if they had placed the child in someone else's care. I had to be the bearer of bad news to the family. He has no money and no insurance, and yet they still looked at me. After I decided to let the state cremate him, suddenly, his oldest living sister came forward and said that she could not allow that to happen. I don't know what the difference was to pay to cremate him or let the state do it for free. One you had the ashes at the memorial the other you didn't. When she made that decision, the cost was then on her. The man that I thought was my father was cremated and memorialized in 2012.

Now, back to my future in Miami. At lunch, he explained what his company did in terms of the services that they were providing their government clients. He also outlined what he was looking for to take his company to the next level. Apparently, from my resume and the initial interview, I was precisely what he was looking for. He asked that I take some time to think about was we discussed and that he would talk to me tomorrow at brunch. For the remainder of the day, he recommended that I destress and enjoy the beach. The next day, I dressed up for brunch, and I am glad that I did because he was dressed to the nines. He took a lot of pride in his style and appearance. Brunch was at a nearby country club in Miami that sat on the golf course. We talked more about the company and what my salary expectation was. I knew that if I was going to leave my government job that it had to be worth it, but I was also considering how unhappy I had been for some time. The number that I had in mind would match my current grade and salary. Instead of me telling him what my salary expectations were at brunch, he requested that I wait, go home and think it over. That is what I did. The next Sunday, it was as if the Woman of God was speaking directly to me, and I clung to every word that she had to say that day. When I got home, I believed that God had confirmed what I needed to do, and I went online to make a post about the Leap of Faith that I was about to take.

I leaped and accepted the role in this small international company. For the next two years, I spent much of my time in Miami. I would be in and out of church due to my schedule. When I would be at church on Sundays suddenly, the Woman of God started to recognize and prophecy on me. Now, all eyes were on me when not a month before that I was slowing dying on the inside. Walking into this new part of my life was just that, I felt as if I had finally gotten out of my wilderness experience. My time away ceased the relationships that I had with the three guys. Big Guy and I had stopped seeing each other before I accepted this position because I wanted more than sushi from him, and he only wanted someone that he could see on occasion.

I had an office space in North Miami with two young ladies that supported me. One was a high school student who was ahead of her time. Some might say that she was a genius graduating at the age of 16, and fluent in 3 languages. It was a rough start with the other young lady and me because of some of the tasks that I was now responsible for significantly depended on her delivery. Later we bonded when she realized that I had her back. I realized that I was a difficult person to work with and began working on how I spoke to her when making requests. You would think that while I was in Miami, I would have spent time at the beach or doing what I love and out dining at the restaurants. Instead of enjoying the beach, I worked. I was in the office before the sun came up and after the sun went down.

These two years flew by, and December of the second year, I started to feel uneasy as if something was going to happen. I reached out to the owner and asked if everything was okay. He responded, "Why would you ask me something like that, Ms. Alston," and I explained that I wanted to make sure that he was still pleased with the support that I was providing. I knew that when I felt this way, nine times out of ten, my instinct was right, but I trusted what he was saying. About three months prior, Baby Girl had accepted a position in New York and was relocating. Her move was costly, and one day while sharing this with the owner, he decided to give me an early bonus of $8000. I appreciated this, and it allowed me to move Baby Girl with ease. Later that month, the owner flew the Miami team and those living outside of the area to Atlanta for a holiday party. I noticed at the party that I wasn't seated with the leadership. I was placed at a table with the employees. I was a Director in the company working at the executive level, so it was unusual for them to seat me with the employees. Only one of the young ladies came from the office, and she did not want to attend, stating that she didn't have the money to travel. The other young lady was going to be traveling with her family for the holidays.

The owner was determined to have the older young lady to attend and rightly so. She was one of his first three employees and had supported him for three years as his executive assistant. I admired her because she relocated to the area from California with no family and friends in Miami. When she arrived in Miami, the owner hired her to support his wife. They also gave her an older model car to drive. Times seemed to be changing now as he was often disappointed in her appearance and would tell me that I needed to talk to her because she was getting fat. He wasn't polite enough to say that she was gaining weight; instead, he said that she was getting fat.

At the holiday party, we were treated differently from most of the people there, but once again, I ignored it. I returned home and didn't know that I would not return to Miami. While at home in discussion with the company recruiter, he had started to have off the record conversations with me where he would advise that I start looking for something else. Honestly, he wasn't clear nor definitive, so although in my heart, I knew that I needed to start looking for something else I had not started. Then on February 2, 2018, it happened, I learned the night before that I would be let go on this day. Angry and disgruntled, I went to the Washington DC office and cleaned it out. I then called the owner and cursed him out. I had also found out that it wasn't just me but my entire Department. I told Baby Girl that morning what I had learned, and she encouraged me, saying, "Don't worry mommy, it will be okay." An hour after I arrived home and sat on the couch, she called me laughing hysterically. When I asked what was going on, she explained that she had just been let go from her position. Neither one of us saw this coming, and instead of her being sad, she could only laugh. It had been three months and two days since she was hired. They explained that they were realigning her position. We later learned that they thought her salary was too high and wanted to pay someone less.

As the day went on, me calling the owner had delayed the inevitable. It was clear the owner was now checking with legal to see what he could and could not do. He had such strict guidelines at his company that we could only refer to each other by our last names to include Mr. or Ms.; this was an oddly strict requirement. During the day, the IT department began to shut off the access to specific systems while the girls still worked. The approach was unprofessional as they had not officially told the ladies that they were going to be terminated. At 5:00 pm, the letters were sent, indicating that we were being released with no real explanation. I learned that this was a result of a $500K financial error in the books but were we the department to cut or should he have cut other areas.

It felt like my life was in disarray all over again. Out of anger, I decided that I would fight by getting a lawyer. Instead of paying one, I used someone that I had started seeing; besides he was one of the original lawyers at the firm that the owner used. It seemed like I had a case at first with the kisses on the cheek, the constant breakfast, lunch, dinner requests, and the comments about the ladies' weight. For this, to work, we needed to stand together. The ladies were young and didn't understand what it meant to fight, so they shied away. I knew the oldest was concerned about money and they had promised one month's pay. I knew that they should have received at least three months of severance, but they didn't know that. After signing the agreement and returning the nearly broken down car that they were allowing the older young lady to drive, and seeing the amount of the check after taxes, suddenly, she understood that we were being treated unfairly, but now it was too late. I ended up helping her pay her rent for a month until she could get back on her feet.

What an unbelievable ridiculously troubling time this was for Baby Girl and me. Two weeks after we both lost our jobs, one Sunday while I was at church, Baby Girl kept calling me back to back, so I knew something was wrong. I stepped out of service, and when she answered, all I could hear was screaming and crying. I didn't know what happened, so my heart immediately sank into my feet, and the strength in my legs gave way. I was squatting because I didn't have the power to stand. I knew that she was planning to attend a church that required that she travel to a different part of the city in New York. I immediately started thinking the worst. The news was heartbreaking, but nothing close to what I was thinking. She began to tell me that Kisses our dog was dying. She had him over half her life; he had grown up as part of our family. I did everything that I could to get there to be by Baby Girls' side. I booked a flight, but by the time I got to the airport, he had to be put down at the Vet and had died in Baby Girls' arms. She had taken such good care of him. Even when he had gone blind being 16 years old, she cared for him like an infant baby. When I arrived, I could see the sadness in her face. I had told the Woman of God and the ministry team why I had left service so abruptly, and they were all concerned and caring. The Woman of God and her Manager checked on Baby Girl and me frequently. Everyone seemed to understand that he was part of the family. I felt like I had a family at the CTR and that I could trust and depend on the Woman of God.

In October, before the department was shut down, I had registered for a conference in Texas, and had not finished paying for the registration. One day while standing in the kitchen, I heard the spirit of God tell me that I should call them and see if I could still pay. I immediately thought that there must be something there that God wants me to see or hear. Maybe the famous Leader would prophesy over my life. Well, I never called. The next day I received an email that said payment is due in full. In my heart, I believed this was God and that he was speaking. Not knowing what I was going to do next, I paid immediately and booked my hotel reservations.

While at the conference, I did not receive a prophecy from the famous Leader. In one of the sessions, he told us to write about what ministry would be like outside of the four walls of the church. At that moment, I received a download and wrote out a complete nonprofit that would include an international ministry. Did God send me there to learn about how to access global opportunities? After the conference, I extended my stay to support a ministry request that the Woman of God received to speak at the P-Mega church in Texas. She allowed me to serve as her armorbearer. This was the first time that I had been granted this opportunity. Although she had started to call me her daughter in Thunder, I was never given the opportunity to serve her in this capacity but watched as she gave it to others. I had not learned my lesson about putting my trust in man and not God. When you don't learn, you must repeat it until you do. I would be lying if I said that I wasn't jealous that she had given this opportunity to someone else because I was. Plainly, she saw how I served, but she would choose someone else. Little did I know it was always part of God's plan.

After I returned from the conference, I felt like I had a new momentum. I started to work with a Lifestylist, had a photoshoot, and filmed a mini movie about my life. I didn't share this with anyone until the YouTube video, my new website, and social media platforms were ready. I shared the concept with the Woman of God after the release because I trusted her feedback and considered her my spiritual advisor. I had chosen the tag Preaching CEO, which I believed highlighted both me being a preacher as well as a CEO. She recommended that I call myself IAMCEO. I decided to stay the course with what was placed in my heart. I launched my new website, ministry, and nonprofit, and it was a success! I had people stopping and asking about my social media and the ministry initiatives. I felt that I had a sense of purpose and direction again. Soon I decided not to move forward with fighting the company for a more substantial severance and to trust that God would provide for me.

In 2018, my responsibilities in the church increased; I was the ministry leader for the Young Adults Ministry, Seniors Ministry, Marriage Ministry, Men's Ministry, and the Women's Ministry. The increased duties added additional conference calls and required more administration. I had some challenges along the way, starting with the leaders of the Seniors Ministry. The Woman of God had requested an end-of-year budget estimate for the following year, and they refused to send them, indicating that was not what they were advised. I responded by sending them an email that I admit should have been worded; differently, it was too formal and direct. I made the statement that they were not going to bully me like they had done the ministry leaders before me. The wife had been difficult to deal with, and I was warned by the front office staff and the former ministry leader. They both advised that she was going to be a challenge. I was determined not to allow her to treat me this way. Because they would not send in their budgets, the Woman of God had to address this matter across the board to get the budgets from everyone. About three months later, I found myself in a meeting with these leaders and the Woman of God. I was so angry I could hardly contain it. The wife refused to listen, refused to submit the required forms, and was blaming it all on me. In the meeting, they brought up the email that I had sent about not allowing them to bully me, but at that time, I had completely forgotten about it and was unable to respond appropriately. If I had, the Woman of God would have known right away that they were the ones that had been holding up the budgets and addressed them directly. Instead, I responded to the wife by saying, "Listen, they warned me about you, and no one wants to work with you." I should never have said that to her in that manner and was glad when the meeting ended. The Woman of God seemed to support me through it all, and I was grateful, but the meeting caused me to digress. It reminded me of being back at my brother's church.

February of that year after feeling the holy spirit unction me to go to service since I had not been most of January when it was time to greet the members a young woman came up to me. She said, "I've been looking for you. The last time you prayed for me, I wanted you to know that everything that you said has come to past". I figured this was why I felt the unction to attend service that day. I believed that God wanted me to see that I was a light in a dark place, but it was more than just that. As I stood there and the Woman of God preached, I felt the Holy Spirit say that I have given her specific instructions as it relates to you, and her time is running out, and tears began to run down my face. The original leader from the Women's ministry that had mentored me for quite some time was standing next to me and put her hands around my waist, saying that God just gave you your answer. She had no idea what God had just told me. Could this be true? Was God telling me to leave? If so, I wasn't ready. Later I requested a meeting with the Woman of God. Unlike others, this would be the first face to face, one on one session that I had with her in the four years of being a member at the CTR. In the meeting that I had with the Woman of God, I explained how I felt about having lost the opportunity in Miami and how it had impacted me financially. We also talked about what ministry looked like for me, for the first time in four years. Was it too late?

Maybe, but I felt like I needed to take the opportunity to talk to her while I was given a chance. On my way there, she called to see if we could cancel, but I was only 15 mins away and begged her to stay at the office. The Woman of God, knew nothing about where I had come from, the church environment, and how God had used me there. I was hoping that this time of sharing would remove what felt like a wall between us. I even shared with her a few visions that God had given me years before coming to the CTR in hopes that she would have some divine insight, but that didn't happen. She did tell me that she would help me as it related to my ministry being international by allowing me to travel with her to Africa. Her ministry outside of the CTR was global. She was well sought after and had crossed many oceans to preach the gospel. I left there thinking that I have a path forward, but nothing ever came of the promises that she made that day.

On a different occasion, I was asked to serve the Woman of God's mentor and spiritual mother. I was both honored and thankful to serve as her armorbearer, and we bonded immediately. She was regal, soft-spoken, and walked in an authority where you knew when she was through the door that she was a woman of God. We exchanged numbers and stayed in touch after that. Whenever she would return to the CTR, I would be asked to serve her again and again.

On another note, I was one of the top givers in the church. They recognized me for my giving over the four years. I was devoted to the success of the ministry, but how was the ministry helping to support my needs? For four years, I had dealt with a lot and kept it hidden under my smile. When I was given the opportunity to speak for a Sunday Easter Service, I was told that I made a significant mistake by coming out too hot when I received feedback from the Woman of God. Instead of taking it as constructive criticism, I took it too heart as a mother scolding her daughter. What I should have heard that she was intently trying to tell me was that I needed to find a point to bring it back down and address the audience. I give the Woman of God credit; she was an excellent teacher; it was just hard for me to deal with the delivery. To my own fault, I was looking for more out of her than I should have. My feelings were hurt that Sunday as she danced and cheered in excitement as others preached, and when I took the platform, she only stared. One of the ladies on my Women's Ministry Team even told me how her assistant went to stand up, and she motioned her not too. I guess this was part of her mean-girl tactics. I wasn't sure, but again my eyes should have been on God and not man. I had ministered many times before and used to be a worship leader, but now I was so intimidated that when I would take the platform, my hands would shake, and I just couldn't get my words right. Intimidation had become my demise! Initially, I didn't have that problem. It developed over time after being told multiple times what I didn't do correctly. It had gotten to the point that I no longer wanted the platform. I had no desire to preside and wanted them to stop asking me. It never failed; she would either walk up behind me just before I went out on the platform to tell me something not to do or reprimanded me after. I felt like the little scolded child in my room, punished and crying to God. These were my issues that needed to be addressed professionally and being there only exacerbated the problem. My Sista friend knew everything, and I always kept her in the loop with how I felt about Ministry and the challenges that I dealt with, and she would do the same. I believed that she was being supportive and had my best interest at heart, so I continued to look at her like the sister that I didn't have. Baby Girl said that we gossiped more than anything, and she proved to be correct. My Sista Friend had been around the Woman of God much longer than I had, but some days it was nearly impossible to tell if she liked her or not. The conversation could go anyway, depending on how she felt that day. So, I agree with Baby Girl. We sat on the phone and gossiped entirely too much. You would think I had learned my lesson from when I was back at my brother's church, but if you look at my track record for not learning from my mistakes, you will be able to understand. You will soon see why I should have been more careful in my conversations. I trusted her and never thought twice that she would betray me, but when a person shows you who they are, believe them.

As the year went on, I started to receive invitations to preach outside of the CTR, and my Sista Friend and another Sista that I had become close with was right there with me. When I returned to the CTR that Sunday, I went to the office to speak to the Woman of God. I decided that I wanted to bless her, and without her asking, I gave her half of what I had received. She asked how the teaching went, and

I explained it all to her. I didn't know anyone there, but they treated me like family. The other ministers were a lot older than me, very seasoned in their Ministry. Some were Pastors, and even one was an Apostle. I wasn't sure what God was doing by placing me among these women, but I trusted God. Before I went to speak, I asked the Woman of God if she had any advice for me, and she said no, go and preach the word. I guess that was good enough for me to go and do what God had called me to do. I wasn't quite sure what was next for me, but every Sunday, it seemed that I become more and more distant from the people at the CTR. One would think that this was impossible with me being responsible for multiple ministries, but I would walk through the doors, not knowing anyone.

I had placed a woman from my original Women's Ministry Team over the Ministry now since I was responsible for overseeing more than one. She had come to me a year before asking me if I could be a mentor to her and how she felt about the Woman of God. The assistant, according to her, had used one of her friends to help ghostwrite her book. I'm telling you gossipers seemed to find me, and here we are again. Come on, no, I hadn't learned my lesson! Most of the things that I have gone through in life were entirely self-inflicted.

Nonetheless, I placed her over the Women's Ministry. She had a rough start and would say how overwhelmed she was, but I encouraged her to stay the course. I believed that she was fully capable, or I would not have selected her. Later, after two ministry events had financial issues, I realized that I had to get more involved with what she was doing, but she did not like the line of questions. As a result, she started to complain about me. One evening, I kept getting email notifications on my phone and opened one not realizing that it wasn't for me. I still had the Women's Ministry email on my phone app. When I saw the email, she was having a conversation with another leader about me; I began to look further. They were going back and forth and with extreme detail. I quickly found out that she was saying that I was rude and unprofessional. She also stated that a ministry event that we had the entire summer was all my idea and how she never wanted to do it. Her accusations were completely inaccurate, and I started to see another side of her that was manipulative. She liked to play sides, which is what she did to me when we met, and she asked if I could mentor her. This woman said that she didn't want the Woman of God to recognize her or to sit on the front row. Deep down, that was all that she ever wanted. I was so tired of the groupie mentality that everyone had. They didn't care about the Woman of God; they merely wanted to be in her face; they wanted the attention. I just wanted to do Ministry. I never shared this with the Woman of God, mainly because I wanted it all to end. I was finished with phony people and, for once in my life, wanted to deal with the matter myself. In November, I had enough more than one person now had turned their back on me. I started to wonder why I was even there. When I arrived at the church, I felt like I was in a place that I no longer knew. A few Sundays after, I was asked to armorbearer the Woman of God's Spiritual mother again. When we came out and sat on the side, I realized that the CTR had drastically changed. The members that initially started with us had moved on. The CTR was now predominately same-sex couples, lesbians, gay men with a few families sprinkled in. The CTR was a safe place to be yourself finally. A place of freedom and love, at least that is what the Woman of God taught. Listen, don't get me wrong; sin is sin. No sin is any worse than the other, so I stand in judgment of no one! The scripture tells us that in Christ, all things are made knew. I believed this based on what God was doing and had done in my life. I decided to go on a fast, the second week in December.

While on the fast the first three days, I didn't hear anything, and on the third night, Baby Girl came into my room and sat on the bed. She said, "Mommy, God is speaking, but you are not listening." I told her that I was listening, and she immediately responded and said, "I pray that God will remove the veil." That night, when I went to sleep, I had a dream, and that morning after waking up, I started to hear God speak clearly. It was time for me to move on. I wanted to wait and talk to the Woman of God face to face, but the Holy Spirit urged me to do it immediately. When I finally spoke to her, I understood why. If I had not sent an email, she would have talked me out of it. I wasn't excited about leaving because I was just licensed and didn't want to be without a church home. That was one thing that I had been trying not to do now since leaving my brother's church, and I had my Sista Friend there.

As always, I shared with her what God told me, and she described what she saw the last time I was an armorbearer for the Woman of God's Spiritual Mother. My Sista friend believed that she was my new spiritual mother and saw a mother coming back for her daughter. She also shared that she thought that I had heard from God. I trusted her and stayed the course. The Woman of God wanted to have a call with me that day. When we talked, I was very emotional, and she explained that I couldn't have heard from God that if God was telling me that he would have informed her first. She asked where I was going, and I told her that I didn't know. God said that he would show me. Again, she explained that God would not lead me out without having another home. I questioned that internally because didn't God do that to Abraham? I know I'm not Abraham, but it proves that God will tell you to leave a place and not show you where you are heading until later. I asked her if she wanted me to give my license back because I didn't want her to think that she licensed me, and now I'm leaving. I was genuinely leaving because God told me too. She immediately said no, I wouldn't ask you to return your license that was God-ordained and not by me.

Chapter 23

Making Amends

At the CTR, we focused on having Triumph in our lives. One area that I was still weak in was my family. I had not talked to my oldest brother, his wife, nor my nieces. The arguments were unforgivable, but we were all God's children and should forgive each other, right? To make amends, I reached out to the family via email. I wanted to take the path of least resistance. Therefore, I sent the email below to my brother's wife on October 10, 2018:

"Hello, I pray that this email finds you well... this email is long overdue, and it's been a struggle for me to write it. One thing that I know for sure is that hurt people hurt people. I apologize for the things that I said, disclosed, and did that changed our relationship. It's been three years, I know, and we have all moved on, but so much has changed and been revealed to me. It's unfortunate that I allowed hurt to make me lash out to hurt those closest to me. It's now evident to me that the entire time I was in Maryland that the enemy was working every angle to move me out. I also know that I went there not because God called me but because my brother said he needed me. Nonetheless, I still have no regrets. Things happen to mold us into who God purposes us to be. When I was confronted in the basement and looked at the hurt in my brother's eyes, it broke my heart, and quite frankly, a light went off inside of me. Then... it was as if the niece that I held so closely in my heart was now the one where it seemed now have turned against me to the point where we both unfollowed each other's posts on Facebook. Then when I made a mistake and had sex because I stopped caring and stopped trying... Although I repented, it continued to weigh so heavy on me that I personally couldn't shake it and shared this with my brother, who condemned me after God had forgiven me. I was sat down from MIT, which I was okay with but then told that I couldn't join the prayer circle, then to step down from the praise team, but I could sing on the choir so I then decided that I would sit myself down from everything. I was hurt, so I decided to take a few Sundays off, but after talking to my brother's wife, and she said, "Why come back," I knew my time was over, so I moved on and never looked back all while carrying hurt. But, what about grace... it was time for me to discover what that really meant for me... And now, I can finally write this email. I've been praying for Victory in five areas of my life, and yet the damaged relationship with my family has not been dealt with. So, I am asking that you will forgive me as I have forgiven you. God is good, and Grace is real. I love you all and pray that you have a Victory Day!"

I wrote the email with good intentions to mend the broken relationships, and unfortunately, I received the below response. I have also included my response to my brother's wife in her email sent on...:

"Hello Tonya,

Let me say that we forgave you three years ago when it happened.

Here we are again. You are sending an email to apologize, but still not dealing with the truth and still pointing fingers. If you were sincere in your heart, you would apologize and move on. So, let me be the one who sets the record straight and speak the truth. I will address everything you mentioned in your email."

My response:

"I expected this because you always think that you are right... We will NEVER see eye to eye, but we don't' have too.

"First, you did not come to Maryland because your brother said he needed you. You came to Maryland because we invited you (and your daughter) to come and live with us because you weren't happy in North Carolina and you wanted a better opportunity for your career."

My response:

"Thanks for pointing this out again as this is ALWAYS your reminder to me how you helped me and MY DAUGHTER! For clarity, I am referring too when I left my home in Virginia to relocate to be closer to the church because my brother said he needed me. Yes, he needed me because you and his relationship had gone to the left. Admittedly you were feeling insecure and thinking you had lost your husband preaching sermons to the women that were offensive like "Don't eat my happy meal" poor **brother's wife**. All while he was calling saying tell **brother's wife** that I'm at your house when he wasn't and fighting for some peace in his home because of your insecurities."

"Also, the niece you said you "Held so closely in your heart," is the same niece you said on Facebook that she was "Not really my niece anyway." It's funny how you forget all the mean and unkind things you said and did on Facebook. Where I could have put all your dirty laundry out there as well, but I didn't."

My response:

"Yes, I apologies for disclosing your TRUTH because that should only have been disclosed by you... As for me and what I have said to Your Oldest Daughter was to lash out on her based what I know she said to me. It was brought to my attention by someone else because neither of us follow the other's post on social media. Anyway, I will not have this discussion with you out of respect for her."

"The "Mistake" you claimed you made by having sex, was not a mistake. Did you forget that you told me how it happened? And yes, God forgives us all our sins, but it doesn't mean you are not going to suffer the consequences of your choices. And no, your brother did not condemn you, he did what any Pastor would have done. You were a minister in sin. Run this one by (my Pastor)."

My response:

"First you are WRONG I stated to you that I was struggling with my flesh. Also, what I told my brother was that he said that "GOD told him that I had sex in November and I asked him three different times" and yet he stood strong on that until I said that is not accurate because I was nowhere near that then. A minister in SIN… WOW what bible are you reading? This is exactly why you are still operating as a store front church. I would also advise you NOT to use her name so loosely! Run this by my Pastor… Well guess what **brother's wife** like I said you can't heal what you conceal, my Pastor and mother in ministry knows how I arrived and why I was there. She has taken years getting all the incorrect doctrine and bad theology out of me. READ YOUR BIBLE! Nonetheless I am the first daughter of thunder, but I hope that everything that you have written makes you feel superior.

"You claim I said, "Why come back." What was the beginning and end of that conversation? You pick and choose parts to make it sound like you are always the victim. I deal in the truth and the truth will make you free Tonya. Stop the lies and half-truths and be free. If you would be honest for a moment you would realize that we did not do anything to you; you did it all to us."

My response:

"Yes you said "Why come back", you also pointed out a response to a question that I had previously asked you… about the comments and non-theological rants that you continued to have in your messages, to say again; You are not all of that, it's not like you have a house on the hill or dripping in diamonds" I recall, stopping you and asking where is this coming from but guess what… It came from your heart because you wanted to remind me again and again don't be thankful for where God has brought you from. Remember Tonya I did that, I brought you into my home, I helped you and your daughter…"

"Let's go down memory lane for a moment. When you were pregnant with Britney, I took you to the doctor when you found out. I also offered you to come stay in Maryland right after because you didn't want to go back to NC to face the abuse of your mother. When you finished college, I (we) offered you the opportunity to come to Maryland to have a better life for you and Britney.

My response:

"Thank you and a person with Christian values of LOVE would not have to keep reminding me of this I have certainly not forgotten but thank you for sharing this with me and everyone that you would like to indulge how you help the poor pregnant girl... and I even heard help pay for my college (LIAR - Interesting **brother's wife**) *So many people have come to tell me what you have done for me and my daughter. Thank you again* **brother's wife** *for helping a poor country girl find her way when she was scared and didn't know what to do!"*

"When you arrived, I saw that I needed to help mold you to be a suitable woman and into the mother that you did not want to be (oh I won't even go into that)."

My response:

"You SAW... okay Thanks **brother's wife** *for trying to be instrumental in the life of a young woman who was taught to be ashamed of getting pregnant at a young age and NEVER told that children are a gift from God and that God is Love. I know that now and made up for lost time with my daughter and she has turned out to be a WONDERFUL WOMAN of God who so dearly wants to heal this relationship. The same young lady that you wanted to help your youngest daughter when she was young and going through depression to help build her self-esteem then later came back and said that your youngest daughter needed to find new friends. The same young woman, my daughter that graduated both High School and College at the top of her class and is both loving and successful. I guess you want credit for that too since I wasn't a suitable woman."*

I tried to help you with the way you dressed and to help you to stop being promiscuous.

My response:

"Thank you **brother's wife** *for trying to press upon me who you thought I should be and not who God created me to be!"*

"I loved you like a daughter, and in my heart, I wanted the best for you."

223

My response:

"Based on this email, I… you want some type of metal or award for your efforts. In your mind, you treated me like your daughter. From what I remember, I paid rent and was always made to feel bad about who I was that I couldn't even share in the success when God started to bless me. Please check you character… You are NOT the woman that you think you are."

"Fast forward. You left the church, again, then you sent an email apologizing and blaming everything on half-sister."

My response:

"I left the church yes, the first time because you and I could not get along. I was bringing Brit up to host the cheerleading practice at the church and because I was unable to attend bible study that week you decided not to inform me that you had canceled the practice. Caring about no one but brother's wife… when I asked what happened, you indicated that if I had been in church, I would have known… So, what, I had to pull an all-nighter on campus trying to finish my MBA but what do you know about that. Then don't forget first lady the voicemail message that you left me… (I, I, I) and I know specifically how I responded! Also as I remember in reference to half-sister, I was outlining the events that took place to make a point of what was said by half-sister that caused the discourse between the two of us and as I recall you added to that conversation… so now was it just me brother's wife come on???"

"You then returned some years later, and as time went on you started to change towards us by starting to spread lies about us, the people who helped you the most. You continued to talk about us to the church members, family members, and to your friends."

My response:

"Not true… but yes, I did return in 2012 and why, because again my bother needed help! I helped get the churches insurance paid and found out how you had been treating him with your insecurities."

"Furthermore, you tainted the women in the church and caused them to leave as well. That said something about them because how could they listen to a sister talk about her brother, who is the Pastor?"

My response:

"Wow so you don't think your rudeness had anything to do with women leaving the church. I'm laughing at this first of all… I was not bashing my family nor my brother and because you are a coward you would never tell me what was said so that I could even respond to the accusations, far as I know you made that up! Women leaving the church… I guess you are talking about C-Bmore. Well let me tell you why C-Bmore left it had nothing to do with me. I was the one making sure that she came to church. Sunday after Sunday I would take my time to go to her house and say come on to service. So why did she leave??? Well she had gone through a series of events and had requested a conference with her Pastor that she never received and she was treated badly by you on multiple occasion at MIT but you know what that's her story to tell but the list goes on and on. Women… well the TRUTH in gossip or story telling it is NEVER done alone. People in your congregation of women came to me to talk. Yes, I admit, in my immaturity I said some things in response that I should have never said but the things that they told me about what you said about me… I swept under the rug and disregarded. Why because I gave you the benefit of the doubt. I know more than what YOU told me about when you caught my brother at Church Member house, cussed her out etc. Sinless minister?!"

"I believe you don't understand true family values. As you know, I have a lot of siblings and we stick together. I would never talk about my siblings to other people and surely not if one is my Pastor. You disregarded the call that God has on his life and the anointing that is upon him. The word says, "Touch not my anointing do my prophets no harm" … surely, he is precious in God's sight."

My response:

"Maybe I don't understand true family values and I certainly don't want to understand the one-sided values that you have. I still remember you telling me on NYE how I didn't need to sit with the family because that was for immediate family…. Well I'm glad you lost some weight and stepped up

225

your game after being insecure about <u>church member</u>. A wife can be replaced but a sister can't!"

"One thing I can say, out of all the women you tainted, you are currently the only one in church trying to fulfill your calling."

My response:

"Really, not sure what you mean by that given you are still struggling like a storefront church…. I am a licensed Rev. with a Masters in Theology and one semester from an earned doctorate. I minister outside of my church so what do you mean by this… again you are sad person **brother's wife** but if it makes you feel better whatever."

"I am glad that you are there with the Woman of God, and eventually you will be totally delivered from the lies."

My response:

"I am glad I am there as well in a ministry that I have been instrumental in supporting for the last four years that has grown leaps and bounds. Where no one was ever concerned about what I drove, my degrees, where I lived nor what I wore. A ministry that was able to purchase .5 million in land in CASH with my help."

The one thing that God hates is a liar.

My response:

"Yep, and without LOVE brother's wife which you lack you are NOTHING to GOD. Read the WORD!"

I pray that you will whole heartedly deal with reality of situations and not be delusional about what really happened between us. This tells me that you have not transformed your thinking. You are still thinking the way you use to think. Thinking negative and being the gossip girl. Think on things that are good, honest and of good report.

My response:

"How much salt do you want to throw, you have always been ALL talk and could barely keep your husband… poor

brother's wife. I was not going to do this I wanted to take a different route LET'S GO! You want the TRUTH, right?!"

> You caused a big misfortune at PLCM then you left to go to another church, when no one knows your real true story or the mess you made at your last church. We were left to clean up the wreak you caused in the body of Christ.

My response:

"Get your facts right... Remember I am anointed by God too. So, if you are throwing stones at me LOOK OUT preacher woman..."

> "Pray for victory in your thinking and accept the wrong that you have done without pointing the finger."

My response:

"I pray the same for your self-righteous attitude and prideful actions that you have."

> "Look at what Tonya has done. You will be judged on what you did, not pointing out what others did! I pray that you will see this email not as a bashing, but advice to help you to be free from the things that so easily besets you."

My response:

"**Brother's wife** you wanted to do what you think you do best and come for me through your words and I should not even be spending my time responding to you but oh well I tried to do what was right with you. Bashing is an understatement you attacked me with your message. Remember the golden rule, a dog that brings gossip will also carry gossip. You first lady participated in the gossip meal as well, shame on you. You know better! The same way that they ran to you they ran to me."

> "Hopefully, one day in our passing we will be able to hug each other and say I love you and keep it moving."

My response:

"This email for me is closure and my attempt to mend what had been broken but I see you speak from the heart. It's unfortunate that you interpreted so much of my original response incorrectly. I also know that you are still jealous since I am still trying to fulfill my calling, but you are right I am… I am trying to be EVERYTHING that God has created me to be an unlike you a copycat of everything original. I will continue to pray for you and keep my distance. I don't want anything to do with the type of person that you are! I wonder, do you see you the way that God see's you."

Be Blessed,

I also included an introduction to my response back to her as quoted above.

"Well… **brother's wife**, I expected you to respond in this manor but not with the extreme lack of accuracy and misinterpretation of my email as you have below, but I guess with only an high school education it can be expected. Some things that my Woman of God and mother in ministry has taught me is that the Moon NEVER barks back at the dog and you can't heal what you conceal. I have spent a lot of time over the years healing despite what you have said below! It's sad that you NEED such a pat on the back and will only see me as the poor pregnant girl that you helped and took into her home. You are a sad subject to say the least."

As you can see from the exchange above, this relationship is not repairable, and to date, I have moved on. Admittedly, I could have done things different. Maybe if I had called her the conversation would have gone another way. Regardless I would have been wrong, and she would have been right. Its best at this point to allow God to take control. I believe that only God could intervene in this matter.

Chapter 24

The Exodus

Departing the CTR, I gave a 30-day notice because I wanted to transition the ministries properly, and the Woman of God decided that we would wait to tell them that I was leaving. I felt bad because most of the ministry teams thought highly of me and had given me a birthday gift as well as beautiful flowers on Mother's Day. I didn't want to leave them without an explanation, so I decided to have a transition period. Looking back now, I should have left the day that I sent the letter. For the remainder of the month, every meeting planned with the ministry department was canceled, which eventually left me with no opportunity to tell the teams the way that I would have liked to inform them. I ended up telling them in January and did not assist with their budget plans as I would have like too. I was told that while the Woman of God was speaking to her Spiritual Mother, she was told by her that there was something in my belly that needed to be birthed out for the CTR. The Woman of God interrupted her to let her know that it was not for the CTR because I was leaving.

That evening I received a call from the Woman of God's Spiritual Mother who asked me why I was leaving, and as I began to explain,

229

I felt as if I was wasting her time and would say to make a long story short when she stopped me to say, no I have time. We spent the next 2½ hours on the phone at the end of the call she explained that she would keep the conversation between us and if I was available to come down to talk to her in person. The next weekend I sought additional counseling from a well recognized leader. The leader mapped out on paper from the first time that I heard God in February about the Woman of God's time running out, until now. The leader concluded at the end that if I didn't leave that I would be disobedient to God. The leader also explained that it was no way that the Woman of God hadn't heard that it was time for me to move on; she just didn't want to believe it. I figured she didn't want me to leave because I would be another top giver that was walking out the door.

In January, due to my travel schedule, I had planned to be at service for three Sundays. At the beginning of the year, there was always a large revival that everyone attended at the megachurch with the Leader from the P-Mega church in Texas. For four years, while at the CTR I was not invited to go with the Woman of God nor offered the ministers upgraded seating for the revival. This year was different. She called with a happy demeanor asking me if I wanted to go with her. I certainly wanted to go and going with her was even better. She knew that this was an undeniable request. Seating was limited due to the high volume of attendees, but as her guest, you would receive VIP seating and treatment. I met her at her house and waited while she got her hair done. When we arrive at the church, I asked her if there were any specific instructions that I needed to know for do's or don'ts. She told me no. As the service went on, the Leader came over and began to pray and prophecy on her, and before I knew she was layed out in the spirt as they call it. I took her shawl and covered her with it, but then there was a rush of women that gathered around her, so I backed away. One of the women was the wife of the Leader. I later heard that she shared with one of the other OTS as she called us, that I left her naked. I have no clue what she meant by that because I was right there the entire time. I would have never put her in a position to leave her uncovered or exposed. After the service ended, there was lunch provided in the back for special invitees. I thought that I was the only one invited until I saw two other OTS come around the corner. She had asked them to go back as well. Her explanation to me, I guess, for her was justifiable. Instead of allowing them in the room where I was with her, she said, "I am taking you into the inner circle, and they will be in the outer circle." I was never moved by these types of things because I wasn't at the CTR for the spotlight that she offered, I came to do ministry, but now I can see how I was sidetracked for so many years. What God was doing was bringing me to a place where I had to trust only him and no one else. God was bringing me into a closer relationship with him, and that could not be done at the CTR and under her shadow.

At the brunch, she asked was there anyone else that I wanted to see after she introduced me to the famous Leader. She believed that taking me into the inner circle was going to make me happy and that I would stay at the CTR. My leaving was based on God and not her. She then went on to say, "You're hurt, aren't you, and I told her no." Later she disappeared and had gone to the other side with the OTS that she sat in the outer circle. I had concluded that we would never have the close relationship that I longed for, but God knew it was time for me to move forward. The next Sunday, when I walked in the front doors, I saw my Sista Friend. She had been acting distant ever since she went to the Woman of God's house for New Year's Eve. I trusted her, so I never asked what was wrong until later.

When I saw her in service, she barely gave me eye contact. I felt that thing that happens in my spirit again that something wasn't right. The Woman of God was starting the service with prayer and had chosen a few members to pray. My Sista Friend was one of them. I guess she didn't tell me because usually, that would have been me praying since I was the Woman of God's back-up for her prayer call when she was out. I wasn't upset at all, and as she began to pray, I prayed quietly in support of her. When my Sista Friend came back to the seat, I rubbed her on her back and said good job.

The Woman of God's message was about me this Sunday, and when she made certain comments, I recall a few of the members that knew I was leaving turned, looked at me, and then I started receiving text messages. As soon as the service was about to end, I left. When I got home that evening, she called and asked if I was okay. I wasn't, but I didn't have the courage to face her and ask why she would preach about me in her sermon.

The next Sunday, I was out of town but received calls about my Sista Friend that she had told a few people that she was happy that I was leaving because she had next. She wanted to be close to the Woman of God, and it was okay, but I never thought that this would happen at my expense. I reached out to tell her what I heard, and she responded that she could say the same about me. We never discussed what was said but I started to see the separation very quickly. I thought we would have been forever Sista's, but I guess not so much. There was another Sista that we both hung out with that had decided to leave the same time that I did, but she never came back after the holidays.

When I attended the next of three services, she preached about me again. This time I sat there and clapped my hands while members texted me. I was prayed up and knew that she would have to answer to God. Why did I keep going back, you wonder? Well, it was because I wanted to keep my word. I felt that I had left my brother's church abruptly and didn't want to do the same for the CTR. I was angry when I walked out and needed to leave before anyone could see the tears that I was holding back. Why was I allowing myself to go through this? I had decided that I wasn't going to attend the last service. Everything in me told me not to go. Baby Girl was home, and I asked her if she would go with me. She didn't want to go, and that morning it was hard for both of us to get dressed and to get there. The only way that I could get her to agree to go with me was that afterward; we would leave to go to her church to see a guest preacher from Australia.

When we arrived at the CTR for my last time, I went to sit on the second row, and the usher came to move my daughter and me to the front row. I noticed that my Sista friend nor any of the other OTS even spoke to me. It was as if I had been outcasted. I thought when someone called you their spiritual daughter; it was supposed to be forever. After we gathered our things to move the front, one of the OTS came and told the usher that we couldn't sit there. I was talking to someone else and didn't hear her, but Baby Girl did and wasn't happy. We sat on the 2nd row, and this time it was evident that the Woman of God was trying to upset me. She brought a OTS on stage that she thought that I was angry about because she moved, yet another ministry from under me and gave it to her. If I were going to be mad about that, I would have been upset long ago. In the four years that I had been supporting this ministry, that was the third ministry where I would get is started and off its feet, and then she would give it to someone else. She had also given this OTS opportunity that she did not allow for me. I will never forget the Sunday that she asked her to speak. They had assigned me to be her armorbearer. When it was time to take her Bible and iPad out, the Woman of God yelled at me to go to my seat and that she would do it. Again, I never knew what I was going to get from her one day to the next. I recall the Woman of God being in Durham preaching at a conference, and my old roommate got in line to meet her. She described her as being rude and obnoxious, and I defended her.

As she preached, there were points in her message that were directed toward me. Baby Girl turned to me and said, "This is why I didn't want to come here." I asked if she wanted to leave, and she said, "No, let's sit right here." So, I sat and looked the Woman of God in her face as she continued to make the points constantly. The Woman of God wanted to hurt me in such a way that she used that OTS to support her message while she made the points about me. We stayed until noon, and as promised, we headed to the next service. As I walked out, I knew that I would never be back. I was making my final exit from the CTR.

I thought my exit would be easy, but it was not without me being embarrassed and the church chatter. I realized that my Sista friend was never a Sista at all, and only a few people reached out to me after my departure. Most of all, the people that use to smile in my face when I walked in the door Sunday after Sunday to serve had distanced themselves from me. The same Sista's that the Woman of God called OTS, that I sat around a lavish, expensive dinner table with me, after organizing a special dinner for our mother in ministry. The same OTS that road in the limo that I paid for out of my pocket to make the Woman of God's night special except for one had nothing else to do with me. Talk about unfortunate! My departure had nothing to do with our sisterhood; it had everything to do with what God was telling me, which was it was time for me to move on. I can't overlook the fact that the CTR had changed a great deal from where we were when we first started. I often felt that the teachings did not emphasize enough that we should be growing in Christ and not remaining the same as we were when we first walked in the door. The purpose of Sunday services was not just to see who could pray the best or who had the best outfit on for the Sunday social media pictures, but it was to be changed. What I saw happening at the CTR was not how we started. Lives were changing in the beginning, the partners as we called them, not members were seeking something that only God could give them. They wanted change, they had hope for something new, and they had strong desires to help others. As a result, ministry events that I was able to plan along with the team's support, resulted in several outreach efforts that helped nonprofits by meeting resource needs for battered women shelters, transition homes, homeless shelters, and orphanages. Was this all in vain? Would I no longer have Sista's or a spiritual mother?

234

When the Woman of God unfollowed me on my social media platforms, I realized that I had my answer. I would no longer call her mother ever again. It was a sad time, as I had spent the last four years serving under her ministry, sharing with her and listening to her intently. I'm not sure that she realized how I valued her as a spiritual advisor, but God knew better. Even after hearing that she had lost her spiritual father, I reached out to her via text, and her response was, "Who is this." The Woman of God has a heavy accent, and I felt like I could hear her virtually ask this question. Regardless, I responded and asked had she deleted my number. It was like my heart had been pierced. I felt like I wanted to cry.

Did I mishear God, was she right? Then she responded and said, "You will always be in my heart." It was too late, the enemy had already planted the seed in my mind, and I wasn't far from right. If she had unfollowed me on social media, she also deleted me from her phone. I later saw her again at a conference in Tampa, Florida, and we made eye contact. In my heart, I was sure that God said it was time to go. Yes, she seemed remorseful when I saw her. I understood why God said to leave now. At a previous conference, not even six months prior, I had taken 15 women to show support. While we were there, I watched how other leaders had made plans for their teams to have seating together. The Woman of God had no idea where we were and enjoyed the spotlight as if the women didn't travel to support her. I called and asked if she would meet the ladies to say hello and take a picture, but she didn't have time. When planning the event, we had promised the women that they would have dinner with her one night, and that didn't happen either. I felt terrible for the women. How disappointing? I did what I would always do and make excuses for her. God decided it was time. Time for me to swim on my own and stand on my own. I had to put my trust in him. Months had passed, and I had accepted it when I saw her face. Yes, God!

Moving with and listening to the voice of God. I would spend the next year visiting churches and attending conferences hoping that God would lead me to the right place. Here I am closing the year, stepping into a new decade without a church home and now finalizing what the holy spirit has led me to do. I am finishing my book. I have re-established my company and launched my nonprofit.

Chapter 25

Rebirth

I am sure you think what a strange name for a chapter, Rebirth. What does this mean? It means that I have been born again. Didn't this happen when you gave your life to Christ, you might ask? Yes, it did, but I have discovered what my Father in heaven has been trying to show me since I was the little girl sitting in my room talking to him and crying. I had found what I have lacked all my life. It was as if, what I have been searching for; I had finally found it in a nearly unexplainable way. It was time for me to STOP nursing the pain!

I had been going to church all my life, raised primarily, in a Christian home. I knew who God was and believed strongly that I could hear from him, but I never surrendered to him. It was always part of me that just held on to what felt comfortable. I lived my life on a roller coaster, not truly accepting, and getting to know who God truly is. I held on to what felt comfortable, the arms of another man. Finally, after more than half of my life, I found Jesus at the well where I had been returning to for so very long. The empty places in my life that I had filled with things, like clothes, shoes, handbags, five-star restaurants, and don't let me forget men. I wanted to be told that I looked beautiful, even when I didn't feel beautiful. I wanted to be touched because it made me feel loved, and I didn't want to be left alone.

What took me so long to get here? Being without a church home has brought me in a closer relationship with God. I recall teaching about the Samaritan woman that met Jesus at the well at a conference called Baggage Check. I understand that before God gives you a word for someone else that I am supposed to be the first part-taker of the gospel. One day while spending my quiet time with God, I opened the alabaster box. Matthew 26:7 (ASV) is a parable about a woman with an alabaster box; it reads: There came unto him a woman having an alabaster cruse of exceeding precious ointment, and she poured it upon his head, as he sat at meat. This woman washed the feet of Jesus with this oil then dried his feet with her hair. It was as if I had finally let go of everything that I had been holding too. I had finally opened up and poured out everything, and I felt God's presence like never before. I felt life breathe into me, and I breathed out what no longer belonged. I felt God's liquid love pour out all over me from the top of my head to the soles of my feet. It was as if he was changing my entire life. I felt warmth, peace, and kindness. His arms of love held me tight as I heard him say, "Daughter I Love You."

"Finally, I realized what he was trying to show me all along. I was not alone, and the love that I had been searching for had been with me all along. Yes, my father was gone, but God was the greatest father of all times. That day I peeled off layers and layers of flesh. I buried clothes that I would never put on again. God had a closet full of new clothes, a robe, and a ring just for me. I know him now like I have never ever known him before. A counselor, A friend, A keeper, and he is with me. Now I truly understand the 23 Psalms and John 3:16; For God so loved the world that he gave. On that day, I gave by dying. I surrendered my flesh to God. I wanted him to live inside of me in a clean temple that I would no longer lay down to another man other than my husband.

The woman that met Jesus at the well was me. She had spent her life in a perpetual cycle doing the same thing again and again with the same results. This was why she kept going back to the well. The parable in John 4:4-26 tells the story of how she came to the well one day like any other, but this time there was a man there that asked her for a drink. I found this parable interesting because here you have a woman with a bucket headed to draw water from a well. Jesus doesn't ask her can I help you draw the water; he asks her for a drink. When I researched this thoroughly, I found that based on measurements taken in 1935, the well was 135ft deep. You would think that Jesus would have offered to help the woman draw from a well of this depth, but instead, he asked her for a drink. He then began to explain that he had something better than what she had been thirsting for. The woman even realizes Jesus to be a prophet, and this was when my eyes opened. She was nothing but a church girl who knew the way. She talked about her ancestors and how they had worshipped on the mount. When I first started this book, I told you about my great aunt, who was a pastor and my mother, who also became a pastor. The Samaritan woman knew the way, just like I had known the way but was still thirsty. What did she lack that she had not found? Jesus asked her to go and get her husband, and she responded that she didn't have one. Jesus agreed and told her even the one that you have now is not your own. Like myself, she had been with many men, and none of them could quench her thirst, so she was back at the well still searching.

I can see myself, all the years that I have searched and tried to please my flesh. My brother's wife would always say, "You always fall to a man." Was I falling to a man or the idea of what I believed to be love? That's it! The Samaritan woman found love at the well. Jesus offered her what no one else could ever offer her, HIMSELF, and he is love. The ultimate gift of love and he hadn't even gone to the cross yet. When this hit me, tears began to run down my face. I knew right then, and this is what I had been looking for, real love. The little girl whose mother never hugged her. The little girl who didn't know who her father was and only wanted his love.

As my healing and rebirth were taking place, I began to listen to an online Pastor Stephen Furtick out of Charlotte, NC. One of the things that stayed with me was right in front of me. As the layers began to peel off one by one, I realized that God had started to give me insight into my greatest vulnerabilities. I realized that because I was not learning my lesson, I had spent much of my life, fighting battles.

I met a young man online; no, I had not surrendered my dating apps. We are all a work in progress, right? Nevertheless, I spent more than two hours talking to him on the phone until I agreed to meet him for coffee. We talked for four hours straight while outside on an early fall day sitting on a bench overlooking the harbor. I told a stranger about my entire life, and I'm still trying to figure out why I shared so much with him, but clearly, this was also part of God's plan. It's such a small world that he knew my brother and had gone to church with him for many years before my brother became a Pastor. As we talked, he looked at me and said, "You stayed in all of those bad situations because you needed validation." I already knew this, right? I'm confident that this wasn't the first time that I had heard this, but you would think that he had told me something profound. I thought I knew that I had this problem, but for some reason, it was as if a light bulb had gone off. Validation… Wow! I believe he is right.

I stayed in those bad relationships because I wanted to make them love me. I stayed in jobs that I hated, where my colleagues and I did not agree, and I was discriminated against because I wanted to make them like me. I stayed at my brother's church because I wanted them to love me. I stayed at the Center because I wanted the Woman of God to see me. It's coming together now. Many of you are thinking, Chile, you should have been figured this out a long time ago! You are RIGHT! I used God as a yo, yo, abusing his Grace. Yes, "We Got Grace," but we should also love God enough to try and do what is right.

I realized that God doesn't change; he changes not. My understanding of God was changing, as my relationship with him had changed. What I know and should have known all along was to listen. I would have avoided the abuse that I endured. There were certain places that I should have stayed away from, not just with my body but with my mind. All those gut feelings that I had been having all my life was God. There was always a voice on the inside saying, "Don't do that, Don't say that, Stop talking so much," and I never listened. Finally, what I know is that the one that created me knew how to counsel me, and all I had to do was listen. Romans 12 teaches us to be transformed by the renewing of my mind. Knowing that I am a work in progress, I realize that I can no longer play with the devil, then turn right around and ask God to deliver me. I will no longer give the devil place, so I have decided to stay away from places that I don't need to be, where my flesh becomes weak. I want to live the life that God has purposed me for and walk in the calling of God. I have let go of the need to prove things to people, let go of the trying to make up for something that I have done in my past. God has already forgiven me. I forgive the abusers in my life that told me that I had ruined my life when I got pregnant, that said to me that I would never be anything. I even forgive my brother's wife, understanding that we may never have a relationship but that we are both God's daughters. I relinquish the control that I allowed others to have over my life both physically and spiritually.

Listening to online pastors and the famous Leader, Yes, the same Leader in my book that in 2019 said that I could call him Papa! I revisited a book that he had explicitly written: "Crushing." I listened to him say, "Those who God crushes the most the more he anoints." The words, spoken by the famous Leader, explains the prophecies over my life, the dreams, visions, and why the enemy has tried to destroy my life. God has anointed me for a mighty work in his kingdom.

Open your heart as you read this story when the Samaritan woman realized that Jesus was all that she needed, she dropped the bucket, which meant she left her past behind. I had finally left my past behind. I refused to be used, manipulated, or taken advantage of any longer. I have found never-ending love. Jesus Loves me despite of me. Despite all the things that I have done in my life. Jesus loves me. Like Mary Magdalene, who some called a whore. Jesus had cast seven demons out of her, and she followed him. Mary became part of the ministry along with the Disciples, and when Jesus rose again, he commanded her to go tell the good news, "Jesus Is Alive!".

When following Jesus, one must understand that to change the fruit; you must first change the tree. I needed and have been undergoing a radical identity change. The word of God tells us that he will make all things new. Before you continue to make excuses for what you do and how you do it, remember. God can and will take off the old and make you new if you surrender and allow him too. Today, I can see Jesus in me. I feel his presence wherever I go, and I hear him when he speaks to me. I've always wanted to dance, and now when I worship in his presence, I see myself dancing beautifully at his throne bowing to feet. I get so teary-eyed; his love is overwhelming me. I don't want to miss my time with him, and when I do, I hear him calling me or saying, "Daughter, you haven't spent time with me today." How can I deny him?

Look at who he is and how he died for me. Beaten, practically tortured, and then executed, for me! I can't get enough of his glory. I want to share the warmth of his arms with everyone that I meet. Jesus is LOVE! I am claiming this as my year of reveal. God is getting ready to reveal who I AM called to be. All the times that the Woman of God, my spiritual advisor walked by and didn't speak. I was never overlooked but hidden. I believe God is moving me from overlooked to can't be missed! God never gave up on me because he knows the plans for my life. He is not looking at my mistakes, only who he created me to be. God deals with the deepest part of who we are that no one knows but him. God looks at the heart and does not condemn us and only wants us to be who he has created us to be. I have been misunderstood my entire life, people have put stuff on me, said that I was someone that was not even me. Now I know that there is no lie that anyone can put on me that will stop what God is going to do in my life. I also know that by writing this tell-all was very risky and opened me up to more reticule.

I am no longer afraid to tell the story of who I am, and where God has brought me from, through, and out of. One thing that I know now for sure is that Jesus has always been with me. We often think that he leaves us because of the terrible things that we may do or how we may live, but God's love will never forsake us. So now I know that he never stopped talking, I just wasn't listening.

Every relationship requires work, and now that I am putting the work in, his love overtakes me. I'm not thirsty anymore for the things of this world; I am only thirsty for his word and love. Guess what? I even deleted my dating apps. I am no longer swiping right. I trust God in this season of my life, and I am enjoying every breath that I breathe. Besides, God knows the plans that he has for me to prosper me and not harm me. The plans to give me hope and a future. I am walking out my every day with Jesus as he turns the pages of my life. Jeremiah 1:5 (ASV) is the confirmation that I need. "Before I formed you in the womb, I knew you. Before you were born, I set you apart and appointed you as my prophet to the nations." It is my time to Go, just like Mary Magdalene, and do what God has anointed me to do. After everything that I have been through, I could have been in prison, dying from an incurable disease, dead from a brain aneurism, or even killed from domestic violence, but God chose to give me a chance. God brought me through Domestic and Spiritual abuse, and there is nothing that God cannot do!

Through it ALL, I am STANDING. I am here, and this is my story TonyaAlstonSpeaks.

About The Author

Founder of TonyaAlstonSpeaks and Healing the Living, organizations that focus on the restoration of lives. Author Tonya Alston has demonstrated that God can bring you out of life-altering situations that you thought you would not make it out of and move you in to your destiny. As a Chief Executive Officer of multiple companies, putting herself and daughter through college, obtaining an International Masters in Business Administration, a Master in Theology, Tonya is not only a leader in the marketplace but for the Kingdom of God as well. Walking in her passion for people, Tonya gathers groups to teach and lead to Christ, and through her nonprofit, she supports battered, displaced women. A native of Washington DC, raised in Wilson North Carolina, Tonya was the 5th daughter of five. She fought through physical, spiritual, and mental abuse, survived a near-death experience, the loss of her mother, and the murder of her Father. Today, Tonya lives in Virginia and is walking in the purposed plan that God has for her life.

CPSIA information can be obtained
at www.ICGtesting.com
Printed in the USA
BVHW040552010520
578756BV00002B/3